In Dedication: _Written and dedicated to Julie Gervasi My wife, partner in ministry, and help. You have always complimented me and make me a better person._

Library of Congress Control Number: 2025908259

The Going Deeper
Study Guide

Frank & Samuel Gervasi

MIDWEST CHRISTIAN PUBLISHING

ISBN: 979-8-998-5125-1-3

Introduction:

Whether you are someone who has a good walk with the Lord or just wanting to draw closer to Christ. Every person of faith finds themselves wanting or needing of a better connection with God. For the person who has drifted, we don't always remember how it happened or how we arrived at that point in our spiritual journey. However, we are all at one time or another, awakened by the realization that we want more of God.

We remember as David did in the Psalms, times where we enjoyed our relationship and our closeness with God. He says, *"These things I remember as I pour out my soul: how I used to go to the house of God under the protection of the Mighty One with shouts of joy and praise among the festive throng." (Psalm 42:4, NIV)* So, we make the decision and commitment to grow in our faith and press hard after God once again. All to experience the thriving faith that we want for ourselves.

Our hope and prayer are that you take these next thirty lessons with the *Going Deeper Study Guide* and be purposeful in pressing hard after God through these *Interactive Lessons*. Each day has a passage that will help the reader be reminded of God's Faithfulness and Goodness. The *Big Idea* for that *Lesson* and passage giving the main point or permanent principle. An *expanded* take-away thought in the *Insight* section with *Application* section. Along with a *Weekly Challenge* and *Prayer* sections to solidify the *Lesson* and growth for that respective *Topic*. Additionally, each *Lesson* includes a *Going Deeper* section that features some writer, commentator, or expanded reference for the day's passage or ideas, along with a *Going Deeper Response Section*.

We hope you faithfully use and enjoy the *Going Deeper Study Guide.*

Going Deeper
Study Guide
by Frank & Samuel Gervasi

Table of Contents:

Lesson 1 - Crowning of the King

Memory Verse: *"I tell you, He replied, 'If they keep quiet the stones will cry out.'"*
Luke 19:40, NIV

Open in Prayer:

Introduction

Every day, when the sun rises over Washington, D.C., it's light first falls on the eastern side of the city's tallest structure, the 555-foot Washington Monument. The first part of this historic monument is to reflect the rising Sun on the eastern side of its aluminum capstone, where one will see the Latin words inscribed, *Laus Deo,* which when translated into English reads, *"Praise be to God."*

Praise is one of the most discussed topics in scripture. In fact, our reading today probably shows one of the greatest moments of worship that Christ experiences on this side of heaven. In our passage, we see the people exalt Christ as King as He rides triumphantly into Jerusalem and give Him the worship He's due. *1*

Read: *Luke 19:35-40*

"They brought it to Jesus, threw their cloaks on the colt and put Jesus on it. 36 As he went along, people spread their cloaks on the road. 37 When he came near the place where the road goes down the Mount of Olives, the whole crowd of disciples began joyfully to praise God in loud voices for all the miracles they had seen: 38 'Blessed is the king who comes in the name of the Lord!' 'Peace in heaven and glory in the highest!' 39 Some of the Pharisees in the crowd said to Jesus, 'Teacher, rebuke your disciples!" 40 "I tell you,' he replied, 'if they keep quiet, the stones will cry out.'" (NIV)

Going Deeper – Study Guide

John MacArthur calls this passage, *"the Coronation of the King," 2* and references it as Christ's last public appearance before His crucifixion. Which I think is an appropriate title for this passage, because it sounds more regal, like a ceremony for royalty. And this was in part, exactly the reason the people of Jerusalem are worshipping with such joy.

1. ***What Other Reasons Could the Crowd Have Been Excited to Worship Jesus?***

_____
_____
_____

In v. 37 it says, *"When he came near the place where the road goes down the Mount of Olives, the whole crowd of disciples began joyfully to praise God in loud voices for all the miracles they had seen."* It was finally time!

2. ***What Barriers Stand in the Way of Keeping a Reverence for the Things of God?***

a. _____
b. _____
c. _____

Consider how they had been hearing about the coming Messiah for so many years throughout the Old Testament readings in the various synagogues. Week after week! Year after year! Reading after reading! They had realized something important: that Jesus was the only true King, worthy of our worship and obedience. And we too need to understand this because how we view Christ and worshipping Him can make a difference.

3. ***What Do the Following Verses Say About Worship:***

Psalm 22:29:	
Psalm 29:2:	
Psalm 55:14:	
Psalm 81:9:	

Big Idea: Always Be Prepared to Worship Jesus –AND Honor Him –as the Only True King

_____

Going Deeper – Study Guide

4. How Can Submission Be Related to Reverence? *(Explain your Answer)*

_____

_____

_____

5. What Areas Do I Need to Submit to God in a Greater Way? *(Explain Your Answers)*

_____

_____

_____

See, the crowd understood that this was a big deal for these people and the time had arrived. They worship Him with their whole heart!

Insight: *Christ Being King Should Mean that a Person Worships Christ in Reverence. However, it Also Means That After We Submit Our Life to Him, -That We Live in Ways That Are Consistent With His Teachings*

6. What Do the Following Verses Show About Submission?

Romans 13:1:	
1 Cor. 14:34:	
Hebrews 5:7:	

"Any Man or Woman on this Earth Who is Bored or Turned Off by Worship is Not Ready for Heaven." A.W. Tozer 3

Going Deeper – Study Guide

What is my general mindset towards praise?

_____

_____

_____

Is it like in the passage? Yes or No (Circle One) (Explain Your Answer)

_____

_____

How can I improve my outlook on praise? _____

_____

_____

Going Deeper:

In this passage, you may notice that Jesus comes into Jerusalem on what some Gospels describe as a *"donkey."* However, Matthew includes the word *foal"* which means that this donkey had never been ridden before. This donkey was one that was supposed to be for the coming Messiah. When Christ did this, He was fulfilling prophecy found in Zechariah 9:9, where it says, *"Rejoice greatly, daughter Zion! Shout, Daughter Jerusalem! See, you King comes to you, righteous and victorious, lowly and riding on a donkey, on a colt, the foal of a donkey."* **4**

Going Deeper Response

USE A BIBLE CONCORDANCE OR BIBLE DICTIONARY AND LOOK UP THE WORDS WORSHIP & REVERENCE FOR STUDY

Pray: Asking God to help us have the same mindset...

_____

Lesson written by Pastor Frank & Samuel Gervasi

_____

1. Wikipedia, https://en.wikipedia.org/wiki/Washington_Monument, as accessed on 11/03/2024.
2. Grace to You, https://www.gty.org/library/sermons-library/81-42/the-humble-coronation-of-king-jesus, as accessed on 11/03/2024.
3. *Inspiring Worship Quotes,* https://mediashout.com/19-inspiring-worship-quotes-2025/, as accessed on 04/08/2025.
4. New International Bible, Holy Bible, New International Version®, NIV® Copyright ©1973, 1978, 1984, 2011 by Biblica, Inc.® Used by permission. All rights reserved worldwide.

Lesson 2 – Membership is Not a Country Club

Memory Verse: *"Consequently, you are no longer foreigners and strangers, but fellow citizens with God's people and also members of his household."*
Ephesians 2:19, NIV

Open in Prayer:

Introduction:

Church membership has been said by some to be a very valuable tool for growing in faith. However, it really has been a misunderstood topic in many churches and believers across the country. In fact, it was recently reported that church membership has gone down 19% in the last sixteen years. Which is really a big number that has ramifications for the Spiritual maturity of many people, including the ones that were not part of this research.

Read: **Ephesians 2:19-22**

"Consequently, you are no longer foreigners and strangers, but fellow citizens with God's people and also members of his household, 20 built on the foundation of the apostles and prophets, with Christ Jesus himself as the chief cornerstone. 21 In him the whole building is joined together and rises to become a holy temple in the Lord. 22 And in him you too are being built together to become a dwelling in which God lives by his Spirit." (NIV)

Big Idea: *Christians become a part of a bigger family, and believers are growing and becoming a Holy Temple where God's Spirit Dwells.*

Going Deeper – Study Guide

The apostle Paul when addressing the church at Ephesus wasn't necessarily correcting any bad or erroneous behaviors, or interpersonal issues with anyone.

Rather he was giving, in part, a sound model for the type of relationships that should exist after a person becomes a Christ follower.

1. What Could Be Some Benefits to Being a Member of a Local Church?

a. _____

b. _____

c. _____

In verse 19 he describes being, "members of Christ's household." Even though he may have been referring to Gentiles being included into God's family, he is also saying that we are *part "of a family with Christ as the head." 2* (verse 20.)

2. Do I View Other Christians as My Family? *(Explain Your Answer)*

_____

_____

_____

Many times, people think that Church membership is not in the Bible. However, the concept is woven through the New Testament and one of the most important tools that God uses to grow us and His church.

Now, the word itself (membership) is not found many times in that form. Nevertheless, in the book of Acts alone, approximately 82% of the passages regarding becoming a Christian are referring to the local body of believers and NOT the Universal Christian Church. There are approximately 17 references to where a person was added to the church. About 14 out of the 17 are giving an image of believers becoming part of a local congregation. That's not counting the epistles where the concept is also being modelled in the context of the local church.

3. What Are Some Benefits to Having People Close to me From Church?

a. _____

b. _____

c. _____

d. _____

4. What Are Some Downfalls to Allowing People Close to Me?

_____

_____

_____

Family relationships are always growing and changing over time. However, ultimately, we become a place where Christ's Spirit can dwell. Verse 29 says that *"we are becoming a holy temple for the Lord."* **1**

Insight: *Membership is a tool that God uses to grow each member into a family. Built on the principles of the Apostles with Christ as the Chief Cornerstone. Membership is a covenant between individual believers and a local church of commitment, where individuals and churches grow into a place where Christ's Spirit dwells.*

Obviously, the Scriptures show the importance of being connected to each other through a local body of believers, even though the actual term might not be there.

5. What Do the Following Verses Show About Families?

John 8:35:	
Acts 7:20:	
Acts 10:2:	
Galatians 6:10:	

Challenge Section:

What mindsets get in the way of being a good member of my local church?

a. _____

b. _____

c. _____

What ways can I grow in the areas I serve?

_____

_____

What ways could hinder God's Spirit dwelling in me?

_____

_____

_____

Going Deeper – Study Guide

Going Deeper:

Member, even though the Greek word is not found in the New Testament. The concept of it is an important one and word. In the Old Testament it may not have been as imperative because Jewish life was centered around the Synagogue. They studied, went to school, served, and were instructed in the Torah. So, the idea of community was almost expected and just assumed. However, in the New Testament the concept of Membership became very important because the church was a new concept. As well as conflict that arose between orthodox Jews and the Christian Church. In fact, some of _"the times that the word is used in the New Testament refers to the organs of a body, as well as a part of the whole."_ Especially in places like Matthew _5:29, Romans 6:13, Romans 7:23, Romans 12:4, and 1 Corinthians 12:12-27._ Which is important because Christ viewed the church as members of a body intricately connected to Himself. _Membership is a covenant between individual believers and a local church of commitment, where individuals and churches grow into a place where Christ's Spirit dwells. **2**_

Going Deeper Response
LOCATE EVERY TIME IN THE BOOK OF ACTS THAT REFERERS TO THE CHURCH & COUNT HOW MANY ARE SPEAKING OF THE LOCAL OR UNIVERSAL CHURCH

**Pray:**   _**Asking God to make my life a place where His Spirit would want to dwell....**_

_____

**Lesson written by Pastor Frank & Samuel Gervasi**

_____

Works Cited:

1.   New International Version (NIV), Holy Bible, New International Version®, NIV® Copyright ©1973, 1978, 1984, 2011 by Biblica, Inc.® Used by permission. All rights reserved worldwide.
2.   J. Knox, An Interpreter's Dictionary of the Bible, Abington Press, Copyright 1962.

Lesson 3 – Benefits of Strong Faith

Memory Verse: *"The Royal Official said, 'Sir, come down before my child dies.' 'Go,' Jesus replied, 'your son will live.'"* **John 4:49-50, NIV**

Open in Prayer:

Introduction:

The dictionary defines faith as: "the ability to trust in the worth or ability of someone or something." 1 However, it really is a great definition even though it's a secular one. Because it relates to matters of faith as well. Both in the concepts of belief in God ---- Himself, and also belief in what the Scriptures tell us as well. Now, in the case of having trust in God, a person needs to accept who He says He is, fully and completely. Additionally, though it's also true because a person must believe completely how the Bible commands, encourages, and exhorts us to live. Nevertheless, that's not such an easy thing to do sometimes, is it? Especially when you think about all the variables that come into play with life at times. Nevertheless, faith is a key ingredient needed for maximum growth regardless of how long a person has been walking with Christ.

Read: *John 4:46-54*

"Once more he visited Cana in Galilee, where he had turned the water into wine. And there was a certain royal official whose son lay sick at Capernaum. 47 When this man heard that Jesus had arrived in Galilee from Judea, he went to him and begged him to come and heal his son, who was close to death. 48 'Unless you people see signs and wonders,' Jesus told him, 'you will never believe.' 49 The royal official said, 'Sir, come down before my child dies.' 50 'Go,' Jesus replied, 'your son will live.'

The man took Jesus at his word and departed. 51 While he was still on the way, his servants met him with the news that his boy was living. 52 When he inquired as to the time when his son got better, they said to him, 'Yesterday, at one in the afternoon, the fever left him.' 53 Then the father realized that this was the exact time at which Jesus had said to him, 'Your son will live.' So, he and his whole household believed. 54 This was the second sign Jesus performed after coming from Judea to Galilee." (NIV).

Big Idea: *Faith is required for all the seasons of a Christ-follower's life if they want to experience God's best in life.*

Faith in *God* **and** His *abilities* is required for **all** of the Christian life, from beginning to end. For both *young* and *old*, both *small* and *big*, -for the newly saved to those who've been following Christ for several years. As well as, from the *smallest* thing, ---to the *biggest* thing we really need God for everything.

If you look at the context of the passage it was very simple for the healing of the Royal Official's son. Even though it doesn't tell us *what* the sickness was, it was definitely a *serious issue* because it says he was *"close to death." (v.47.)*

1. **Do I believe God Heals in Dramatic Ways like in the passage?** _____
_____
_____

2. **What Mindsets/Thoughts Get in the Way of Having Faith That God Can Do the Miraculous in My Life?** *(Be Thorough)*
    a. _____
    b. _____
    c. _____

What's clear is that the official believed **fully** that Jesus could do the miraculous in his son's life. Because v. 47 says *"He went and begged"* 2 Christ for healing. Now, it could have been out of *desperation*, but most likely, it was because he had heard and maybe even seen second hand about all Christ had been doing. The miracles performed, the teaching with authority, and even challenging long held beliefs of the leaders of that day and culture.

Even Though God *Cares* About *Everything*—Christ's *First* Concern is a Person's *Soul*. Consider that, because He doesn't care more about your *health* than your final destination. He doesn't care about your *wealth* more than your soul. And He doesn't care about your *relationships* more than the place in eternity either!

What Jesus **does** care about *most* is whether you've come to a place of repentance, and whether you've received the forgiveness that comes from embracing the Cross. (John 3:16.)

3. *Why Would God Care So Much About a Person's Soul?* _____

_____

_____

Insight: *Belief is really required for all needs in the Christian life. If you have a need, trust fully that God can do whatever is needed for you. Whether it's a minor relationship issue, are facing a major decision, or are at the receiving end of a major health scare.*

4. In What Ways Do I Limit God in My Life? (Explain Your Answers.)

a. _____ b. _____

b. _____ d. _____

In verse 48 it *says* *"'Unless you people see signs and wonders,' Jesus told him, 'You will never believe.'"* *2* Even though Christ doesn't say that specifically, that is what was being referred to. Because the *signs and wonders* that people would see, were just the signs that He was the Son of God, that was to come into the World. The Kingdom of God had finally arrived.

5. What Do the Following Verses Say About Faith?

Genesis 5:24	
Genesis 17:1	
2 Chronicles 20:20	
Mathew 6:30	
Luke 5:20	

"If you believe in a God who controls the big things, you must believe in God who controls the little things. It is we of course to whom things look little or big." 3 Elliott

Going Deeper – Study Guide

What is My Level of Faith Currently? (Rate Yourself 1-10-Explain Your Reasoning)

_____

_____

_____

What Areas Have I Allowed My Faith to Weaken?

_____

_____

_____

What Practical Things Can I Do to Grow in Faith?

a. _____

b. _____

c. _____

Going Deeper:

There's also another reason that shows the Royal Official had great faith. And that is, _because_ he was said to have worked for Herod Antipas, the son of Herod the Great. Even though that doesn't sound like it's significant.it really is! Because he was _most likely_ **not** very fond of Christ ---being raised around all that _jealously and animosity_ towards Christ. In fact, Pilate sent Christ back to Antipas, and he was mocked and sent back and forth. So, the Royal Official that was asking for a miracle was used to hearing nothing but negative talk about Jesus. All that to say, that he was showing great belief in who Christ was saying that He was! The **NIV Study Bible** adds "_unless you see signs and wonders you will never believe." Was the general attitude of Galileans, not that of the official." **4**

Going Deeper Response

READ HEBREWS 11 - HALL OF FAITH CHAPTER, AND LIST EVERY PERSON THE WRITER BRINGS UP FOR HAVING FAITH.

Pray: _Asking God to stretch my faith in Him, so that I can experience Him in a greater way...._

_____

Lesson written by Pastor Frank & Samuel Gervasi

_____

1. Webster's Dictionary, Merriam-Webster, Inc, 2016
2. New International Version (NIV), Holy Bible, New International Version®, NIV® Copyright ©1973, 1978, 1984, 2011 by Biblica, Inc.® Used by permission. All rights reserved worldwide.
3. Jungle Pilot, Russel Hilt, Discovery House Publishers, 1997
4. NIV Study Bible, BibleGatewayPlus, Biblegateway.com, as accessed on 03/20/2025

Lesson 4 – Praying Like a Disciple

Memory Verse: *"One day Jesus was praying in a certain place. When he finished, one of his disciples said to him, 'Lord, teach us to pray, just as John taught his disciples.'" Luke 11:1, NIV*

Open In Prayer

Introduction:

Our prayer life is probably one of the most important things that we can do! That true because it's one of the most basic disciplines for the Christian, and every follower needs to do it. But prayer can be one that is also a misunderstood and under-taught topics in some churches. Additionally, it doesn't matter how long you've been a Christian because no one seems to graduate from the necessity of prayer. Christ himself, realized the importance of it and prayed often. You see prayer is the thing that makes our faith real. It takes us from just mere head knowledge to actually living out the Christian faith. Some people pray often - and for long periods of time, but for others, it's small, short, one-line prayers - as they're going about their day. However, both types of people understand the importance of praying on a regular basis.

Read: *Luke 11:1-4*

"'One day Jesus was praying in a certain place. When he finished, one of his disciples said to him, 'Lord, teach us to pray, just as John taught his disciples.' 2 He said to them, 'When you pray, say: Father, hallowed be your name, your kingdom come. 3 Give us each day our daily bread. 4 Forgive us our sins, for we also forgive everyone who sins against us. And lead us not into temptation.'"
(NIV)

__Big Idea:__ Prayer is Critical and Should Be Inspiring When Pray Like a True Disciple

Going Deeper – Study Guide

The passage we are studying today is between an encounter between Jesus and His disciples regarding prayer. They had all been influenced and experienced Jesus praying daily and in various ways and with various requests. (v. 1.) So, after finishing one day his disciples ask to be taught about prayer. (v.1.) They had also experienced John the Baptist pray, as well as teach his own followers. There must have been something compelling about seeing Jesus pray or they probably wouldn't have asked. If you think about it: They grew up going to the synagogue, so they had seen people pray often. Meaning, it wasn't foreign to them. In fact, they had probably grown up and were accustomed to praying.

1. **What Are Some Possible Reasons People Can Sometimes Avoid Prayer?** *(Explain & Give an Example)*

_____
_____
_____

2. **What Do the Following Verses Say About Prayer?**

Exodus 9:29	
1 Samuel 2:1	
2 Samuel 7:27	
Romans 1:10	
Romans 12:12	

3. **What Specific Areas Can We Pray For?** *(Explain Your Answers)*

a. _____ b. _____

c. _____ d. _____

One of the most popular prayers in scripture is what's known as the Lord's Prayer. Which is exactly what Christ chose to teach His disciples when asked to be taught as John the Baptist's disciples were taught. (v. 2.) *However,* giving a model or standard for prayer as opposed to actual prayer to be verbatim. In verse 2 he says: *"Father, hallowed be your name,"* [1] showing that we should remember who we are coming before when we pray. *"Thy kingdom come,"* implying that we should be longing for God's kingdom to be realized here on Earth during our lifetime. And prayer should also be for daily provision in life, (v.3,) when he says, *"Give us this day our daily bread."* As well as forgiveness when we fail, or others fail us. In v. 4 it says: *"Forgive us our sins, for we also forgive everyone who sins against us."* [1] As well as praying for strength against life's temptation (v. 4.)

I was taught the same prayer at a young age. I always knew the words, but something seemed to be missing in the reciting of the Lord's Prayer. The actual pattern that was behind it seemed to be replaced with repetition of the words only.

Insight: *Consider having a prayer life that others want to emulate. It is probably one of the most encouraging things that shows our prayer life, when done correctly, can inspire others and be contagious.*

---

4. When is Your Ideal Time and Format to Pray? (Explain Why and Give An Example)

_____

_____

_____

John Bradford the English Reformer, prebendary of St. Paul's, and martyr said that, when he was in prayer, he never liked to rise from his knees till he began to feel something of brokenness of heart.

"Get up to your chamber, hen, if you would have a broken and contrite spirit and come not out until you have it." John Bradford 2

Challenge:

What is my prayer life like currently? _____

_____

_____

Do I spend regular time before God's throne, or not? _____

_____

_____

How can I continue to grow in prayer? _____

_____

_____

Going Deeper – Study Guide

Going Deeper:

The Greek term father as used in the New Testament is an understood one to the audience that Luke was reaching initially. However, the term Abba was probably more well known.

Abba was Aramaic in origin and said to be a term of endearment and closeness. So, for Jesus to use it, may have been saying that we can come freely and abandon ourselves before God the Father when we bring our requests. Even the ***Zondervan Illustrated Bible Backgrounds Commentary of the New Testament*** addresses that: *"While it has been commonly said that Abba is a children's term meaning "daddy," this is not quite right, since Jewish adults also addressed their parents in this way. Abba was, however, a term of considerable intimacy. While Jews would sometimes refer to God as "our heavenly Father," they rarely if ever addressed him as "my father" or "father" (Abba). Jesus calls his followers to a new intimacy with God through his unique relationship with the Father." 3*

Going Deeper Response
USE A CONCORDANCE AND DO A SEARCH FOR PRAYER. LIST 5 REFERENCES THAT PERTAIN TO TRANSPARENCY BEFORE GOD

Pray: Asking God to stretch my prayer life, so that I can experience Him in a fresh way....

―――――――――

Lesson written by Pastor Frank & Samuel Gervasi

―――――――――

Works Cited:

1. New International Version (NIV), Holy Bible, ® Copyright ©1973, 1978, 1984, 2011 by Biblica, Inc.® Used by permission. All rights reserved worldwide.
2. Sermon Central Contributor, www.sermoncentral.com, as accessed on 03/20/2025
3. Zondervan Illustrated Bible Backgrounds Commentary of the New Testament, Copyright © 2002

Lesson 5 - Trust and Obey

Memory Verse: *"So, Abraham called that place The Lord Will Provide. And to this day it is said, 'On the mountain of the Lord it will be provided.'"* ***Genesis 22:14, NIV***

Open in Prayer:

Introduction:

Sometimes, obedience is costly and defies logic. During the Prussian siege of Paris in the late 1800s, there was a gunner in one of the French forts named Pierre Barlot. One day, Pierre was standing by his gun when General Noel, his commander, said to him, "Gunner, do you see the Sevres bridge over there?" "Yes, sir." "And that little shanty in a thicket of shrubs to the left of the bridge?" "I see it, sir," said Pierre. "It's full of Prussians, I believe; try it with a shell." Pierre turned ghostly pale. He sighted his cannon carefully, then fired it, and blew the hut to shreds. The commander Noel praised Pierre for his marksmanship but was surprised to see a single tear running down the gunner's cheek. "What's the matter, man?" "Pardon me, General," said Pierre, "it was my house—everything I had in the world." 1

Read: *Genesis 22:1-18*

"Some time later God tested Abraham. He said to him, "Abraham!" "Here I am," he replied. 2 Then God said, "Take your son, your only son, whom you love—Isaac—and go to the region of Moriah. Sacrifice him there as a burnt offering on a mountain I will show you." 3 Early the next morning Abraham got up and loaded his donkey. He took with him two of his servants and his son Isaac. When he had cut enough wood for the burnt offering, he set out for the place God had told him about. 4 On the third day Abraham looked up and saw the place in the distance. 5 He said to his servants, "Stay here with the donkey while I and the boy go over there. We will worship and then we will come back to you." 6 Abraham took the wood for the burnt offering and placed it on his son Isaac, and he himself carried the fire and the knife. As the two of them went on together, 7 Isaac spoke up and said to his father Abraham, "Father?" "Yes, my son?" Abraham replied. "The fire and wood are here," Isaac said, "but where is the lamb for the burnt offering?" 8 Abraham answered, "God himself will provide the lamb for the burnt offering, my son." And the two of them went on

Going Deeper – Study Guide

together. 9 When they reached the place God had told him about, Abraham built an altar there and arranged the wood on it. He bound his son Isaac and laid him on the altar, on top of the wood. 10 Then he reached out his hand and took the knife to slay his son. 11 But the angel of the Lord called out to him from heaven, "Abraham! Abraham!" "Here I am," he replied. 12 "Do not lay a hand on the boy," he said. "Do not do anything to him. Now I know that you fear God, because you have not withheld from me your son, your only son." 13 Abraham looked up and there in a thicket he saw a ram[a] caught by its horns. He went over and took the ram and sacrificed it as a burnt offering instead of his son. 14 So Abraham called that place The Lord Will Provide. And to this day it is said, "On the mountain of the Lord it will be provided." 15 The angel of the Lord called to Abraham from heaven a second time 16 and said, "I swear by myself, declares the Lord, that because you have done this and have not withheld your son, your only son, 17 I will surely bless you and make your descendants as numerous as the stars in the sky and as the sand on the seashore. Your descendants will take possession of the cities of their enemies, 18 and through your offspring[b] all nations on earth will be blessed, because you have obeyed me." (NIV)

Big Idea: *Faith in God, proven by deliberate and complete obedience, will always be compensated in due time.*

God commanded Abraham to show a similarly great depth of faith in what some have called Abraham's "final exam". There was no softening of the blow when God spoke to Abraham clearly in verses 2-3: *"'Take your son, your only son, whom you love – Isaac – and…sacrifice him there as a burnt offering.'"*

Don't forget how everything that God had promised Abraham about his descendants was going to be fulfilled through Isaac. Isaac was himself a miracle, considering the age at which Abraham and his wife Sarah gave birth to him. Then God is asking Abraham to sacrifice the child who was the very fulfillment of His promise years earlier.

1. **What Does it Mean to Sacrifice Something?** (Explain Your Answer) _____
   _____
   _____

2. **What Do You Think God Wants you to Sacrifice to Grow in Faith?** (Be Specific)
   a. _____ b. _____
   c. _____ d. _____

What God asked Abraham to do does not sound, in our day and age, like good fatherly advice. In fact, you might receive a visit from Family Services for child-rearing like this! And yet, Abraham responds with deliberate, decisive, and complete obedience. Notice that Abraham rose "early the next morning" (v. 3). Abraham did not hesitantly delay doing what

God said, he was quick and decisive to trust and obey from the moment God told him to sacrifice Isaac, his own son!

3. Look Up the Following Verses and Write Down What Character Trait Stands Out?

Genesis 3:13	
Psalm 109:16	
Proverbs 23:24	
Luke 11:11	

Additionally, Abraham is tested for his faith in this passage. He believes God at His Word and trusts Him fully, and, in response, God rewards Abraham for his faith. First, God provides a way out of the demanding situation by providing a ram in a thicket *"caught by its horns"* (v. 13) to be sacrificed in Isaac's place. At the very last moment, when Abraham is about to go through with the unimaginable, God provides a way out.

Insight: *Faith and obedience are inseparable: one cannot claim to take God at His word if he or she is not willing to do what God has said. When we say that we have faith in God, we must obey His commands.*

4. What Are Reasons Obedience Can Be Hard at Times?

a. _____ b. _____

c. _____ d. _____

Then finally, God Himself rewards Abraham's faithfulness by renewing the covenant in verses16-18: *"'I swear by myself, declares the LORD, that because you have done this and not withheld your son, your only son, I will surely bless you and make your descendants as numerous as the stars in the sky...and through your offspring all nations on earth will be blessed, because you have obeyed me.'"*

5. Look Up the Following Verses and Describe How God Responded to Their Faithfulness?

Genesis 15:1	
Numbers 22:17	
Ruth 2:12	
1 Samuel 26:23	

Psalm 19:11	
Colossians 3:24	

God may never ask us to trust Him for something so great. But He does ask all of us, at various times, to trust Him for something. And complete faith, proven by obedience, will always be compensated in due time.

Challenge

What Areas of My Life is God Asking Me to Have Faith With? _____

_____

_____

What can I Do to Grow in Trusting and Obeying God? _____

_____

_____

*What Have I Been Withholding from God?*_____

_____

_____

Going Deeper:

In Hebrews 11, the Hall of Faith, Abraham is one of those commended for his faith in verses 17-19: *"By faith Abraham, when he was tested, offered up Isaac; and he who received the promises was offering up his only begotten son; it was he to whom it was said, 'In Isaac your seed shall be called.' He that considered that God is able to raise men even from the dead."*

The **NIV Study Bible** says regarding these verses:
"If you are afraid to trust God with your most prized possession, dream, or person, pay attention to Abraham's example. Because Abraham was willing to give up everything for God, he received back more than he could have imagined." **2**

Pray: Asking God to help me trust Him no matter the circumstances and obey fully no matter how difficult.

Going Deeper Response

FIND A BIBLE COMMENTARY AND LOOK UP GENESIS 22:1-18

Lesson written by Pastor Frank & Samuel Gervasi

1. Ministry127, https://ministry127.com/resources/illustration/the-cost-of-obedience, as accessed on 08/25/2024.
2. Zondervan NIV Life Application Study Bible. Ronald A Beers, gen. ed. Zondervan. Copyright 2011

Lesson 6 – Forgiveness is Not Optional

Memory Verse: *"Then Peter came to Jesus and asked, 'Lord, how many times shall I forgive my brother or sister who sins against me? Up to seven times?'"*
Matthew 18:21, NIV

Open in Prayer:

Introduction

Just before Easter in 2009, Fred Winters, pastor of the First Baptist Church in Maryville, Illinois, was shot and killed during a Sunday morning service by a disturbed young man. The tragedy shocked the church and the pastor's family, but it did not destroy their faith. The next week the newly widowed Cindy Winters was interviewed on a national news broadcast. When asked about her husband's killer she said, *"I do not have any hatred or even hard feelings toward him. We have been praying for him."* [1] We may never have to forgive someone for something so tragic, but we are **ALL** called to forgive at one time or another.

Read: *Matthew 18:21-35*

"Then Peter came to Jesus and asked, 'Lord, how many times shall I forgive my brother or sister who sins against me? Up to seven times?' 22 Jesus answered, 'I tell you, not seven times, but seventy-seven times.' 23 'Therefore, the kingdom of heaven is like a king who wanted to settle accounts with his servants. 24 As he began the settlement, a man who owed him ten thousand bags of gold was brought to him. 25 Since he was not able to pay, the master ordered that he and his wife and his children and all that he had be sold to repay the debt. 26 'At this the servant fell on his knees before him. "Be patient with me," he begged, "and I will pay back everything." 27 The servant's master took pity on him, canceled the debt and let him go. 28 'But when that servant went out, he found one of his fellow servants who owed him a hundred silver coins. He grabbed him and began to choke him. "Pay back what you owe me!" he demanded. 29 'His fellow servant fell to his knees and begged him, "Be patient with me, and I will pay it back." 30 'But he refused. Instead, he went off and had the man thrown into prison until he could pay the debt. 31 When the other servants saw what had happened, they were outraged and went and told their master everything that had happened. 32 'Then the master called the servant in. "You wicked servant," he said, "I canceled all that debt of yours because you begged me to. 33 Shouldn't you have had mercy on your fellow

servant just as I had on you?" 34 In anger his master handed him over to the jailers to be tortured, until he should pay back all he owed. 35 'This is how my heavenly Father will treat each of you unless you forgive your brother or sister from your heart.'"

__Big Idea:__ Forgiveness is not optional and costly and will require something of us to pardon others when they have hurt us.

In today's Bible passage, we see a parable where Peter asks Jesus an important question regarding forgiveness. *"Then Peter came to Jesus and asked, 'Lord, how many times shall I forgive my brother or sister who sins against me? Up to seven times?'"* (v. 21, NIV) Even though it sounds like a straightforward question, it may have been rooted in what was taught during those times. The main teaching by Jewish leaders regarding forgiveness, was that a person could be forgiven up to three times to fulfill Mosaic Law. So, for Peter to ask up to seven times may have been a way to seem *ultra-spiritual* before his mentor.

1. How Easy, or Difficult, Is It for You to Forgive Someone When They Have Wronged You? *(Explain)*

_____

_____

_____

However, Jesus raises the bar for His followers by giving such a large number. In verse 22 it says that, *"Jesus answered, 'I tell you, not seven times, but seventy-seven times.'"* Which was an even bigger number than what many were used to hearing. Implying that God doesn't want us to keep track of how many times we forgive others.

2. What Might Be Some Reasons It's Difficult to Forgive Someone Multiple Times for the Same Offense? *(Be Specific)*

a. _____

b. _____

c. _____

Additionally, another aspect regarding forgiveness is that it usually will cost us something when a person makes the choice to forgive an offense. Whether that hurt is just the financial cost of a real debt, or an emotional debt from being hurt.

In the parable, Jesus tells of a king that wanted to settle an account of a servant that owed him about twenty years of a day-laborer's wages and could not pay (vv. 23-24). Nevertheless, when the servant could not pay the debt and he begged the king to forgive the debt, he was released (v. 25).

Going Deeper – Study Guide

3. What Do the Following Verses Say About Forgiveness:

Genesis 45:4-7:	
2 Samuel 19:18-23:	
1 Kings 21:27-29:	
Micah 7:18:	
Ephesians 4:32	

4. What Might It Cost Us to Forgive Others? *(Explain your Answer)*

_____

_____

_____

_____

Insight: Forgiveness will cost a person something, and we should reciprocate to others like our heavenly Father forgives us – avoiding hypocrisy...

When the servant was put in a similar situation, for an even smaller amount, he did not forgive the person who was indebted to him. Instead, he went and had him thrown into prison until the debt could be paid, as we see in verses 28-30, *"But when that servant went out, he found one of his fellow servants who owed him a hundred silver coins...'Pay back what you owe me!' he demanded...But he refused. Instead, he went off and had the man thrown in prison until he could pay the debt."*

5. Why Might We Fail to Show Forgiveness to Others? *(Explain Your Answers)*

_____

_____

_____

_____

Jesus paid the price for our forgiveness with the high price of death on a Cross. We should also reciprocate and forgive others!

Going Deeper – Study Guide

6. What Do the Following Verses Show About God's Forgiveness Toward Us?

Psalm 103:12:	
Nehemiah 9:17:	
John 3:17:	
Romans 5:8:	

"What sets Christians apart from the world is the obligation and compulsion to forgive."
Author Unknown

Challenge Section

Who do I need to forgive for an offense? _____
_____
_____

Do I give out forgiveness freely, or tend to withhold it? Yes or No (Circle One) (Explain Your Answer)
_____
_____
_____

Am I keeping count of when someone wrongs me? _____
_____
_____

Going Deeper:

The Talmud, which was the central rabbinic teaching for Judaism, instructed that people were to forgive up to three times. However, after that there was no longer an obligation to forgive another individual. At least in what was required when obeying Mosaic Law. The **NIV Grace and Truth Study Bible** says, *"Within Judaism, forgiving someone three times was enough to show a forgiving spirit (Job 33:29–30; Am 1:3; 2:6). Peter's suggestion of seven times shows generosity. Jesus' response is not about a specific number but is an instruction to forgive without keeping count.*
He illustrates this with a parable in which a servant owes his king an incalculable debt, at least 2.5 billion dollars in today's terms. The point is the immensity of the debt and the

impossibility of paying it back. The king orders that the servant and all he has be sold into debtor's slavery, a common practice in the ancient world that was designed both as a punishment and as a means to repayment (cf. 2Ki 4:1; Ne 5:4–8)." [2] Additionally, some versions of the Bible say seventy-times-seven which is a large number, even much more generous than the seven times Peter suggested. However, some manuscripts suggest that it was seventy times seven which is four hundred and ninety times.

Going Deeper Response
USE A BIBLE CONCORDANCE OR BIBLE DICTIONARY AND LOOK UP THE WORD FORGIVENESS FOR STUDY

Pray: Asking God to help us forgive no matter the circumstances and not matter how many times we have been hurt...

_____

Lesson written by Pastor Frank & Samuel Gervasi

_____

Works Cited:

1. Ministry127, *https://ministry127.com/resources/illustrations/forgiveness,* as accessed on 3/20/2025.
2. *NIV Grace and Truth Study Bible*, Copyright © 2021 by Zondervan, 2011. *BibleGateway Plus*, www.biblegateway.com, as accessed on 3/20/2025.
3. New International Bible, Holy Bible, New International Version®, NIV® Copyright ©1973, 1978, 1984, 2011 by Biblica, Inc.® Used by permission. All rights reserved worldwide.

Lesson 7 – Enduring Prayer

Memory Verse: *"'Ask, and it will be given to you; seek and you will find; knock and the door will be opened to you.'"* **Matthew 7:7, NIV**

Open in Prayer:

Introduction

A fisherman was at sea with his godless companions when a storm came up and threatened to sink their ship. His friends begged him to pray; but he said, *"It's been a long time since I've done that or even entered a church."* At their insistence, however, he finally cried out, *"O Lord, I haven't asked anything of You in 15 years, and if You help us now and bring us safely to land, I promise I won't bother you again for another 15!"*

Unfortunately, many people view prayer as an escape mechanism rather than a constant line of communication with God. **1** Prayer is necessary for our relationship with God. However, when the answer is long in coming, we should still continue to pray.

Read: *Luke 18:1-8*

"Then Jesus told his disciples a parable to show them that they should always pray and not give up. 2 He said: 'In a certain town there was a judge who neither feared God nor cared what people thought. 3 And there was a widow in that town who kept coming to him with the plea, "Grant me justice against my adversary." 4 'For some time he refused. But finally he said to himself, "Even though I don't fear God or care what people think, 5 yet because this widow keeps bothering me, I will see that she gets justice, so that she won't eventually come and attack me!"' 6 And the Lord said, 'Listen to what the unjust judge says. 7 And will not God bring about justice for his chosen ones, who cry out to him day and night? Will he keep putting them off? 8 I tell you, he will see that they get justice, and quickly. However, when the Son of Man comes, will he find faith on the earth?'"
(NIV)

Big Idea: We should be persistent in prayer and never give up even when the request is a long time in being answered.

1. Who is Someone You Know Who Never Gives Up? _____

_____

_____

The passage we're looking at is from the Gospel of Luke. And in it, Jesus was teaching about never giving up in prayer, and how to persevere over time when we need to. So, He does this by telling a parable to make His point, involving an unjust judge and a widow. So, there are many variables that come into play as well.

First, Jesus was teaching a parable to His disciples. However, He was obviously speaking to all people who call themselves Christ followers and would later read this. Additionally, we also know that parables are stories used to teach spiritual truth. So maybe they happened, maybe not, but it doesn't really matter anyway when it comes to applying them to our lives.

2. What Might Be Some Reasons God Takes So Long to Answer Our Prayers?

a. _____

b. _____

c. _____

We saw that the story contained some main characters, like a judge, a widow, and an unnamed adversary. (vv. 1-3.) We read in v. 2 *"That there was a certain judge who neither feared God nor cared about men."* Which I think says a lot about this judge's mindset because he really didn't seem to care about what this widow even needed. That mindset is much different than our God because He is One who cares intimately about all that concerns us always.

However, something that I think stands out is the widow's request. Because Luke records the term *"adversary"*. Verse 3 says: *"And there was a widow in that town who kept coming to him with the plea, 'Grant me justice against my adversary.'"* One version uses the word *opponent* – which is an interesting word because it actually carries this idea of an opponent much like in a lawsuit. Which explains why she was going to a judge in the first place: to seek justice from the unjust judge. (v. 2.)

3. What Do the Following Verses Show Us About Prayer:

1 Kings 18:41-45:	
Ezra 8:23:	
Jeremiah 33:3:	
John 15:7:	
Colossians 4:2:	

Nevertheless, the Judge was not fair or even concerned about the people in general. So why would this judge help the widow?

egardless of the details, he did grant her request because of her tenacity and persistence. (vv. 5.) ""Even though I do not fear God nor respect man, yet because this widow bothers me, I will 've her legal protection, otherwise by continually coming she will wear me out.""" (NASB 1995)

4. What Might We <u>Not</u> Pray with Persistence When the Answer Is a Long Time in Coming? *(Explain your Answer)*

_____
_____
_____

Insight: We should pray with determination and perseverance because it keeps us focused on the need, especially when the answer is long.

So, if the unjust judge will grant justice, how much more will God hear the prayers of His children? God longs to give His best to us, so we should come freely and with abandon before His throne.

5. How Might It Look for Us to Pray with Abandon? *(Explain Your Answers)*

_____
_____
_____

"We should pray, then pray more, and after that pray even more." Author Unknown

We may not need a judge to decide a case for us, but we all have needs of one variety or another. Regardless of what those are, endurance is usually needed, and we would be wise in being persistent in prayer.

6. What Do the Following Verses Show About God Answering Our Prayers?

Psalm 18:6:	
Proverbs 15:29:	
2 Chronicles 7:14:	
Mark 11:24:	

Going Deeper – Study Guide

On a scale of 1 to 10, how persistent am I in prayer? (1 being the lowest, 10 the highest)

1 – ---------------2.5----------------- 5 -------------------7.5------------------10

Do I easily give up when the wait is long? Yes or No (Circle One) (Explain Your Answer)

_____

_____

_____

What are some ways I can train myself to be persistent in prayer? _____

_____

_____

Going Deeper:

Consider the widow in the parable because they were said to be very needy in that time and culture. Much different than today because widows are very independent and do many things for themselves. In fact, we have widows today, and they take care of themselves perfectly fine. However, in that day, widows were very dependent on others just like in this parable. One source says: *"The widow was a helpless person with nothing but right on her side. She wanted justice, not revenge."* (ESV Reformation Study Bible, Ligonier, 2015) **2**

Additionally, the **Expositor's Bible Commentary** says, *"The theme is that of the vindication of God's misunderstood and suffering people. God's people in the OT days needed to "wait" on God as he worked out justice with apparent slowness (see Ps. 25:2-3). In the final days the martyrs wait for vindication (Rev 6:9-11). Meanwhile we wrestle with the problem of evil and with issues of theodicy. Under these circumstances we should 'always pray and not give up.'"* **3**

Going Deeper Response

USE A BIBLE TO LOOK UP THREE CHARACTERS IN THE SCRIPTURES WHO PRAYED PERSISTENTLY. READ THEIR STORIES, AND WRITE DOWN THE LESSONS YOU CAN LEARN ABOUT PRAYER FROM THEIR LIVES.

Pray: Asking God to give us the endurance we need to pray over the long haul when needed...

Lesson written by Pastor Frank & Samuel Gervasi

Works Cited:

1. Ministry127, *https://ministry127.com/resources/illustrations/prayer,* as accessed on 3/20/2025.
2. *ESV Reformation Study Bible,* Copyright © 2015 by Ligonier. *BibleGateway Plus, www.biblegateway.com,* as accessed on 3/20/2025.
3. *Expositor's Bible Commentary* (Abridged Edition): New Testament, Copyright © 2004. BibleGateway Plus, *www.biblegateway.com,* as accessed on 3/20/2025.
4. New International Bible, Holy Bible, New International Version®, NIV® Copyright ©1973, 1978, 1984, 2011 by Biblica, Inc.® Used by permission. All rights reserved worldwide.

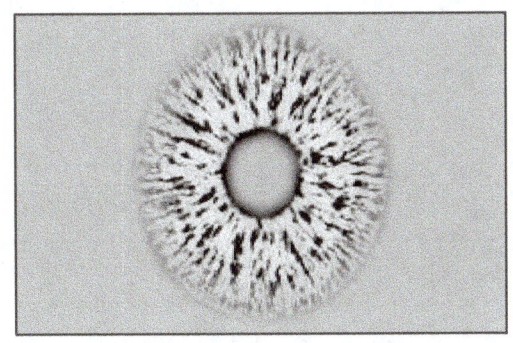

Lesson 8 – Eye in the Sky

Memory Verse: *"The LORD will watch over your coming and going both now and forevermore."* **Psalm 121:8, NIV**

Open in Prayer:

Introduction

King salmon, also known as Chinook salmon, lead an incredible life. After spending most of their lives in the ocean, Chinook salmon embark on a migration back to the same freshwater streams where they were born to lay their own eggs. This journey often covers several thousand miles and requires the salmon to swim against the strong force of the current. Yet every year, thousands can be seen swimming in a caravan to go back to the place they were born.

The Israelites often made a similarly difficult journey, albeit of a shorter distance. Every year, the Israelites would come up from all their towns and villages to the temple in Jerusalem for the annual feasts. The road was often long and difficult, and there were dangers of inclement weather, wild animals, and bandits along the way. Consequently, during this journey, it was customary for the travelers to sing a "song of ascent" – one of fourteen psalms specially designed for these travelers. Our psalm today is one of these "songs of ascent", and in our passage we will learn some valuable things about God's watchful care over us.

Read: _Psalm 121_

"I will lift up my eyes to the mountains; From where shall my help come? 2 My help comes from the Lord, Who made heaven and earth. 3 He will not allow your foot to slip; He who keeps you will not slumber. 4 Behold, He who keeps Israel Will neither slumber nor sleep. 5 The Lord is your keeper; The Lord is your shade on your right hand. 6 The sun will not smite you by day, Nor the moon by night. 7 The Lord will [a]protect you from all evil; He will keep your soul. 8 The Lord will [b] guard your going out and your coming in From this time forth and forever." (NIV)

Going Deeper – Study Guide

Big Idea: God's watchful care is reliable, tailor-made, and motivated by His love for us.

1a. What Do You Think of When You Hear the Words "Dependence" or "Depend On"?

_____

_____

_____

OR

1b. What is the biggest road trip or journey you have ever been on?

_____

_____

_____

For the journey the psalmist is about to embark on, his dependence on God is clear to see in verses 1-2: *"I lift my eyes up to the mountain – where does my help come from? My help comes from the LORD, the Maker of heaven and earth."* Notice that the Psalmist doesn't depend on his own knowledge as his source of strength; he doesn't turn to money or place his trust in a government official. The writer is confident and convinced that his help comes from the Living God, the *"...Maker of heaven and earth."*

2. For what reasons is depending on God worthwhile?

a._____

b._____

c._____

From our passage, we see three reasons for the psalmist's confidence in God. For one, the Psalmist knows that God's assistance is reliable, as we see in verse 3: *"He will not let your foot slip; he who watches over you will not slumber..."* This is a great image, when you think about it, because people get tired and run down, and our bodies are made to need rest. But God is not limited by these restrictions. He never grows tired or weary (Isaiah 40:28-31); His care is reliable and never lacking!

3. **What Do the Following Verses Say About God's Reliability:**

Deuteronomy 31:8:	
Psalm 20:7:	
Psalm 55:22:	
2 Thessalonians 3:3:	
Hebrews 13:8:	

4. **What Does It Look Like for a Person to Place Their Confidence in God?** *(Explain your Answer)*

_____

_____

_____

The Psalmist also recognizes that God's care is tailor-made. In verse 5, the Psalmist makes the distinction that, *"The LORD watches over you..."* Implying that God's care is specific to us and our lives.

5. **In What Areas Do I Need God's Special Tailor-Made Help in My Life?** *(Explain Your Answers)*

_____

_____

_____

Insight: When God is watching over a person, He will provide exactly what is needed in life, because nothing is hidden from His sight. He knows every detail of our lives; therefore, we can trust His watchful care.

Then, finally, the writer trusts God's care because it is motivated by love. Look again at v. 8: *"The LORD will watch over your coming and going both now and forevermore."* God's love never weakens or fades, and it will watch over us forever.

7. **What Do the Following Verses Show About God's Loving Care?**

Psalm 32:7:	
Matthew 11:28:	
Romans 8:38-39:	
1 Peter 5:7:	

Going Deeper – Study Guide

Many people turn to many different things for strength and comfort in life. Some are valid and make sense, and some don't. But we, as children of God, have the best place to turn when life gets hard or we find ourselves in a confusing situation. The God of the universe intimately cares for and has His eye on us.

Challenge
To what or whom do I tend to turn when I need assistance?
_____
_____
_____
Do I come to God first and foremost, or is He my last resort? _____
_____
_____
How can I learn to trust God's care in my life? _____
_____
_____

Going Deeper:

Many believe this psalm was written by King Hezekiah, the 13th ruler of the southern kingdom of Judah in the Old Testament. Throughout his reign, Hezekiah was responsible for nationwide spiritual reform, because they had become a people who had grown apathetic toward the things of God. Hezekiah's leadership sparked national revival, as the people reopened the doors to the Temple and put aside their idols. Hezekiah was said to have a close relationship with God, which I think is evident because you can tell that he relied fully on God for help – just like we should!

The **Bible Knowledge Commentary** also says this about songs of ascent: *"The title 'song of ascent' identifies each of Psalms 120-134 as a pilgrim song to be sung when the Israelites 'ascended' (went up) to Jerusalem for the annual feasts. Four of these 15 psalms are ascribed to David (Ps. 122; 124; 131; 133), 1 to Solomon (Ps. 127), and the other ten are anonymous...The pilgrim-psalmist [in Psalm 121], as he contemplated his journey through the hills to Jerusalem, asked where his help came from. He found the answer to his question*

Going Deeper – Study Guide

> USE A BIBLE COMMENTARY AND LOOK UP THE PSALM 121.

in the affirmation of his faith that the LORD, who created heaven and earth – with those hills – was his only Source of help," **1**

Pray: Asking God to help me trust the help He provides and not rely on my own understanding or strength...

_____

Lesson written by Pastor Frank & Samuel Gervasi

_____

<u>Works Cited:</u>

1. Walvoord, John F. and Zuck, Roy B. "Psalm 120-A Contemplation of the Journey", from *The Bible Knowledge Commentary*, SP Publications, Inc., 1985, pg. 882-883.

2. New International Bible, Holy Bible, New International Version®, NIV® Copyright ©1973, 1978, 1984, 2011 by Biblica, Inc.® Used by permission. All rights reserved worldwide.

Lesson 9 – "Grace in Action"

Memory Verse: *"When they persisted in asking him, he straightened up and said to them, 'He who is without sin among you, let him be the first to throw a stone at her.'"* ***John 8:7, NIV***

Open in Prayer:

Introduction:

I heard a story once about a pastor who, one Sunday morning, found the roads to his church blocked. Due to this unexpected obstacle, he was forced to skate on the river to get there. When he arrived, the elders of the church were horrified to learn that their preacher had skated on Sunday – the Lord's Day!. After the service they held a meeting where the pastor explained that it was either skate to church or not go at all. After a pause, one elder asked, "Did you enjoy it?" When the preacher answered, "No," the board cleared him of wrongdoing. **1**

Read *John 8:1-11*

"But Jesus went to the Mount of Olives. 2 At dawn he appeared again in the temple courts, where all the people gathered around him, and he sat down to teach them. 3 The teachers of the law and the Pharisees brought in a woman caught in adultery. They made her stand before the group 4 and said to Jesus, "Teacher, this woman was caught in the act of adultery. 5 In the Law Moses commanded us to stone such women. Now what do you say?" 6 They were using this question as a trap, in order to have a basis for accusing him. But Jesus bent down and started to write on the ground with his finger. 7 When they kept on questioning him, he straightened up and said to them, "Let any one of you who is without sin be the first to throw a stone at her." 8 Again he stooped down and wrote on the ground. 9 At this, those who heard began to go away one at a time, the older ones first, until only Jesus was left, with the woman still standing there. 10 Jesus straightened up and asked her, "Woman, where are they? Has no one condemned you?" 11 "No one, sir," she said. "Then neither do I condemn you," Jesus declared. "Go now and leave your life of sin." (NIV)

Big Idea: *Grace looks beyond the letter of the law to a person's heart, bringing forgiveness, restoration, conviction, and change.*

In our passage today, we find a similarly legalistic group of Pharisees bringing before Jesus a woman caught in adultery. From verse 6, we learn that, *"They were using this question to trap him..." and* make Him say something that would discredit His reputation. Instead, Christ responded with wisdom, and modeled to us the mindset we should have when it comes to grace.

1. **Why Can Showing Grace Come hard sometimes?** *(Explain Your Answer)*

_____
_____
_____

2. **What Do the Following Verses Say About the Law?**

Deuteronomy 4:4:	
Deuteronomy 5:1:	
Deuteronomy 6:25:	
Deuteronomy 7:11	
Deuteronomy 8:11:	

The adulterous woman's accusers were *"the teachers of the law and the Pharisees"* (v. 2), both of which went to great lengths to follow Mosaic Law. In fact, these religious leaders were correct in what Mosaic Law prescribed regarding the punishment for adultery (v. 5). However, they completely threw mercy and compassion out the window in the process, and their real intentions behind this episode were dishonest and self-serving.

But whereas the religious leaders condemned the woman for her failure, Jesus responds with grace: *"When they persisted in asking him, he straightened up and said to them, 'He who is without sin among you, let him be the first to throw a stone at her.'"* (v. 7)

Going Deeper – Study Guide

3. **Rate Yourself in Showing Compassion. 1 (Lowest) – 10 (Highest).**
   1 _____ 2 _____ 3 _____ 4 _____ 5 _____ 6 _____ 7 _____ 8 _____ 9 _____ 10 _____

4. **What Areas Do You Find it Hardest to Show in Compassion in?** *(Why. Explain)*
   a. _____ b. _____
   c. _____ d. _____

Insight: *Grace not only pardons and forgives us but causes us to pursue holy living. When we understand the power of grace, we don't want to abuse it in any way. Grace should always produce change and lead us to something better.*

He didn't have to do a lot, did He? Jesus' question itself brought conviction to the religious leaders and caused them to evaluate their own lives. And in response, *"...they began leaving one by one..."* (v. 9), for none present could claim that they had never sinned.

5. **What Do the Following Verses Show About God's Grace?**

Zech. 2:10:	
John 1:16:	
Acts 11:23:	
Acts 14:3:	
Romans 5:15:	

In the end, only Jesus and the woman remained. Notice how he didn't yell at her or attack her. He didn't ask, "What's wrong with you? I can't believe you fell again!" Instead, *"...Jesus said, 'I do not condemn you either. Go. From now on, do not sin any longer.'"* (v. 11) Some versions translate it as, *"'Then neither do I condemn you. Go now and **leave your life of sin**.'"* It was the grace that was shown that day that probably changed that woman forever!

The same is true for us. It is ultimately the grace that God has shown to us that acquits us of our wrongdoings, forgives us, empowers us, and prompts us to change. And because it was freely shown to us, we should show it to others as well! I heard one person say it like this:

"The people who tend to be the most gracious are those who know how badly they need grace." Unknown

Challenge:

HOW MIGHT I SEE THE POWER OF GRACE THAT CAUSES CHANGE IN MY OWN LIFE?
_____
_____
_____

HOW CAN I GROW IN GRACE? _____
_____
_____

HOW CAN I SHOW GRACE TO OTHERS? _____
_____
_____

Going Deeper:

Warren Wiersbe once said this: *"We must not misinterpret this event to mean that Jesus was easy on sin or that He contradicted the law. For Jesus to forgive this woman meant that He had to one day die for her sins. Forgiveness is free, but it is not cheap. Furthermore, Jesus perfectly fulfilled the law so that no one could justly accuse Him of opposing its teachings or weakening its power....The law was given to reveal sin (Rom. 3:20), and we must be condemned by the law before we can be cleansed by God's grace. Law and grace do not compete; they complement each other. Nobody was ever saved by keeping the law, but nobody was ever saved by grace who was not first indicted by the law. There must be conviction before there can be conversion." 2*

Going Deeper Response

FIND A BIBLE CONCORDANCE AND LOOK UP GRACE. WRITE DOWN HOW MANY ARE CONCERNING PEOPLE SHOWING GRACE. AND HOW MANY CONCERN GOD SHOWING GRACE: GOD: _____
PEOPLE: _____

Close in Prayer Asking God to Show You How to Extend Grace to Others.....
_____

Lesson written by Pastor Frank & Samuel Gervasi
_____

1. Today in the Word, Moody Publishers, December 1989, p. 12
2. Warren Wiersbe, Copyright © Warren W. Wiersbe.

Lesson 10 – Learning to Speak Wisely?

Memory Verse: *"For if we could control our tongues, we would be perfect and could also control ourselves in every other way."* **James 3:2b, NIV**

Open in Prayer:

Introduction:

A husband and wife tell a story about how recently they *"sat down to eat in a local restaurant."* And the husband, *"had gone to the restroom and when the server came over to get our drink orders, my wife said, 'We'll both have water, and I'll have iced tea. I don't know what he'll drink.' The server responded, 'So what's he going to do with the water?'"* 1

Our words are powerful and can be used in a positive but also negative way causing harm if not careful. In our passage today, in the book of James. It's one where he compares our speech with three different things, a fire, a ship, and a horse. And each one has something in common, a small thing having a big effect.

Read: **James 3:1-12**

"Not many of you should become teachers, my fellow believers, because you know that we who teach will be judged more strictly. 2 We all stumble in many ways. Anyone who is never at fault in what they say is perfect, able to keep their whole body in check. 3 When we put bits into the mouths of horses to make them obey us, we can turn the whole animal. 4 Or take ships as an example. Although they are so large and are driven by strong winds, they are steered by a very small rudder wherever the pilot wants to go. 5 Likewise, the tongue is a small part of the body, but it makes great boasts. Consider what a great forest is set on fire by a small spark. 6 The tongue also is a fire, a world of evil among the parts of the body. It corrupts the whole body, sets the whole course of one's life on fire, and is itself set on fire by hell. 7 All kinds of animals, birds, reptiles and sea creatures are being tamed and have been tamed by mankind, 8 but no human being can tame

Going Deeper – Study Guide

the tongue. It is a restless evil, full of deadly poison. 9 With the tongue we praise our Lord and Father, and with it we curse human beings, who have been made in God's likeness. 10 Out of the same mouth come praise and cursing. My brothers and sisters, this should not be. 11 Can both fresh water and saltwater flow from the same spring? 12 My brothers and sisters, can a fig tree

Big Idea: *Our Speech is Powerful! –So, We Should Use Caution When We Speak.*

---

bear olives, or a grapevine bear figs? Neither can a salt spring produce fresh water." (NIV)

Even though our tongues are a small part of our bodies, our words can have big effects, can't they? And we can use them for good, or we can allow them to destroy and hurt other people. We saw in verse 5: *"Even so the tongue is a little member and boasts great things."* Even though James uses the word tongue he's obviously referring to our speech, the words we say and the things that come out of our mouths. What comes out of our mouths when we interact with those around us, ---matters to God.

1. **Why Should Our Speech Matter?** *(Explain Your Answer)* _____

_____

_____

2. **Have You Ever Been Hurt by Someone and What They Said?** (Explain How You Felt?)

_____

_____

_____

James describes our tongue as something small but powerful in verse 5b-6: *"A small thing that makes grand speeches. But a tiny spark can set a great forest on fire."* I think it's an excellent picture when he's talking about our speech. Because some of the World's largest and most destructive forest fires all started with one spark.

3. Look Up the Following Verses and Write What Stands Out?

Job 15:3:	
Psalm 19:3:	
Proverbs 8:13:	
Ecc. 5:13:	
Acts 5:40:	

Going Deeper – Study Guide

Nevertheless, even though it's difficult we can't use it as an excuse because God still wants us to use our speech in a way that honors Him. So, we need to learn to discipline our speech, regardless of the difficulty.

4. Why Do You Think Speech Be Difficult for People? (Explain Your Answer) _____

_____

_____

_____

Insight: *Even Though it's Difficult Our Speech Should Be Mastered - So We Can Live Wisely!*

_____

_____

5. What Times Are Speech Difficult to Control for You? (Explain Your Answer) _____

_____

_____

_____

If we look starting in v. 7, James likens our speech with all the various animals that have been tamed by man. However, our speech being very difficult to master. *"For every species of beasts and birds, of reptiles and creatures of the sea, is tamed and has been tamed by the human race. But no one can tame the tongue; it is a restless evil and full of deadly poison."*

6. Look Up the Following Scripture and Write What Stands Out About Our Words?

2 Cor. 8:7:	
1 Timothy 4:12:	
Titus 2:8:	
1 Peter 3:10:	

God cares about how we use our speech, and our words should be controlled because they are powerful. So, we should learn to use our speech in ways that build others up and encourage them.

Going Deeper – Study Guide

I heard one person say: *"you can tell a person's character by the words he or she uses!"*
(unknown)

Challenge:
HOW MIGHT I USE MY SPEECH TO BUILD OTHERS UP AND NOT TEAR DOWN? _____ _____ _____ HOW CAN I SPEAK IN AN EDIFYING WAY? _____ _____ _____ WHO DO I NEED TO APPOLOGIZE TO FOR MY SPEECH? _____ _____ _____

Going Deeper:

The term here *"perfect"* in verse 2 is not referring to absence of fault. However, it is speaking of the *"spiritual maturity"* that Christians should be striving for. The **NIV Study Bible Notes** also confirms and expands on this important word by saying that if a person could tame their tongue, it would most likely filter over into other areas of their life as well. *"Since the tongue is so difficult to control, those who control it perfectly gain control of themselves in all other areas of life as well. James indicates that complete control of the tongue, if it were possible, would render a person 'perfect.' This reflects the same Greek term from 1:4, where it indicates 'maturity.'"*

Even though it is difficult, we should learn to master our speech in a way that helps and _not_ hurts others. **Ephesians 4:29** is the standard that was set by the apostle Paul as well when he says: *"Let no [a]unwholesome word proceed from your mouth, but only such a word as is good for edification [b]according to the need of the moment, so that it will give grace to those who hear." 2*

Going Deeper Response
CFHOOSE A PERSON YOU CAN CALL AND ENCOURAGE THIS WEEK AND INVITE TO CHURCH AND A CUP OF COFFEE

Going Deeper – Study Guide

Pray: _Thanking God for the ability to use my speech in a good way. Asking for the power I need to master it…._

_____

Lesson written by Pastor Frank & Samuel Gervasi

_____

Works Cited:

1. Speaker Stories, https://speakerstories.wordpress.com/2012/04/16/people-are-funny/, as accessed on 03/20/2025.
2. NIV Study Bible, Copyright © 1985, 1995, 2002, 2008, 2011 by Zondervan.

Lesson 11 Confidence in God

Memory Verse: *"But joyful are those who have the God of Israel as their helper, whose hope is in the Lord their God."* **Psalm 146:5, NIV**

Open in Prayer:

Introduction:

There is a story about a father who went rock climbing with his son, Zac. The two were out in the country, climbing around in some cliffs, when the father heard a voice from above him yell, "Hey Dad! Catch me!" He turned around to see Zac joyfully jumping off a rock straight toward him. He had jumped first and then yelled "Hey Dad!" Things became an instant circus act, as the father moved into position to catch him. Both fell to the ground. When the father found his voice again, he gasped in exasperation: "Zac! Can you give me one good reason why you did that???" He responded with remarkable calmness: "Sure...because you're my dad." 1

We all place our trust in someone or something. Many times, we choose to trust other people, expecting them to be looking out for us. In some situations, that trust is well-placed, like with Zac and his dad. But other times we place our confidence in the wrong people for the wrong things. As we'll see in our devotion today, there is only one Person in whom we should be placing our ultimate confidence. And we should be overflowing with thankfulness when we realize just how reliable He is.

Read: Psalm 146

"Praise the Lord. [a] Praise the Lord, my soul. 2 I will praise the Lord all my life; I will sing praise to my God as long as I live. 3 Do not put your trust in princes, in human beings, who cannot save. 4 When their spirit departs, they return to the ground; on that very day their plans come to nothing. 5 Blessed are those whose help is the God of Jacob, whose hope is in the Lord their God. 6 He is the Maker of heaven and earth, the sea, and everything in them— he remains faithful forever. 7 He

Going Deeper – Study Guide

upholds the cause of the oppressed and gives food to the hungry. The Lord sets prisoners free, 8 the Lord gives sight to the blind, the Lord lifts up those who are bowed down, the Lord loves the righteous. 9 The Lord watches over the foreigner and sustains the fatherless and the widow, but he frustrates the ways of the wicked. 10 The Lord reigns forever, your God, O Zion, for all generations. Praise the Lord." (NIV)

Big Idea: *We should never place our confidence in people but rather give our trust and worship to God.*

Last week, we saw how Psalm 146 exhorts us to worship joyfully before God, and in these verses, we now see one of the reasons we should give God that praise: people fail, but God does not. Look at vv. 3-4: "*Don't put your confidence in powerful people; there is no help for you there. When they breathe their last, they return to the earth, and all their plans die with them.*"

1. **Describe the Difference Between Worship & Praise?** _____
_____
_____

2. **What Are Common Things People Place Their Confidence in?** (Expand on Your Answers) _____
_____
_____

We can see something clearly in these verses: God may be worthy of our adoration, but people will never measure up in the same ways. And that will be true of even the best, wisest, most respectable person we could know. They will still always be lacking, because they will always be limited to what extent they can help us.

3. **Look Up the Following Verses and Discover What They Say About God?**

2 Samuel 22:4:	
1 Chronicles 16:25:	
Psalm 18:3:	
Psalm 96:4:	
Matthew 3:11:	

4. *What Are Reasons God is Worthy of Our Praise?* (Be Specific)

a. _____ b. _____

c. _____ d. _____

Verse 3 describes *"powerful people"* or some versions say *"princes"*. We can all picture someone who fits this description – someone with influence and status. Nevertheless, even these people will let us down at one point or another.

But isn't it good news to know that God will never let us down? Look at the contrast between vv. 3-4 (which we read earlier) and vv. 5-6: *"But joyful are those who have the God of Israel as their helper, whose hope is in the LORD their God. He made heaven and earth, the sea, and everything in them. He keeps every promise forever."*

Insight: *Trust and praise have a symbiotic relationship. When we choose to place our confidence in God, we are moved to worship Him. Likewise, when we worship God even in the harshest trials, we find it easier to have faith in God's perfect plan.*

---

5. *How Do the Following Verses Describe God?*

Deuteronomy 33:29:	
Psalm 10:14:	
Psalm 27:9:	
Hebrews 13:6:	

Even the most trustworthy people on earth will fall short and fail us, but we serve the never-failing God of Armies. How should we respond? The psalmist responds in jubilant praise! Throughout the rest of the psalm, he demonstrates his thankfulness and gratitude for the faithfulness and reliability of his King. Let's offer our trust and affection to God as well and choose to place our confidence in Him rather than fallible human beings. And let's worship joyfully before the Lord!

6. *What Things Do I Have to Be Grateful to God for*? (Explain Your Answers)

a. _____

b. _____

c. _____

Challenge:

WHERE HAVE I BEEN PLACING MY CONFIDENCE? _____
_____
_____

WHAT DO I NEED TO TRUST GOD WITH TODAY? _____
_____
_____

WHY HAVENT I TRUSTED HIM IN THESE AREAS? _____
_____
_____

Going Deeper:

Matthew Henry, in his Commentary on the Whole Bible, says regarding verses 3-4: *"David is supposed to have penned this psalm; and he was himself a prince, a mighty prince; as such, it might be thought...that he himself, having been so great a blessing to his country, should be adored, according to the usage of the heathen nations, who deified their heroes, that they should all come and trust in his shadow and make him their stay and strong-hold. 'No,' says David, 'Put not your trust in princes (Ps. 146:3), not in me, not in any other; do not repose your confidence in them; do not raise your expectations from them. Be not too sure of their sincerity; some thought they knew better how to reign by knowing how to dissemble. Be not too sure of their constancy and fidelity; it is possible they may both change their minds and break their words.' But though we suppose them very wise and as good as David himself, yet we must not be too sure of their ability and continuance, for they are sons of Adam, weak and mortal. There is indeed a Son of man in whom there is help, in whom there is salvation, and who will not fail those that trust in him."* **2**

Going Deeper Response

MAKE A GRATITUDE LIST ABOUT THE TANGIBLE WAYS GOD HAS PROVIDED AND HELPED YOU THIS PAST YEAR.

Pray Thanking God for All the Ways He Helped you in Life.....

Lesson written by Pastor Frank & Samuel Gervasi

---

1. Adapted from https://www.sermonillustrations.com/a-z/t/trust.htm; as accessed on 11/20/2024

2. Matthew Henry's Commentary on the Whole Bible, public domain.

Going Deeper – Study Guide

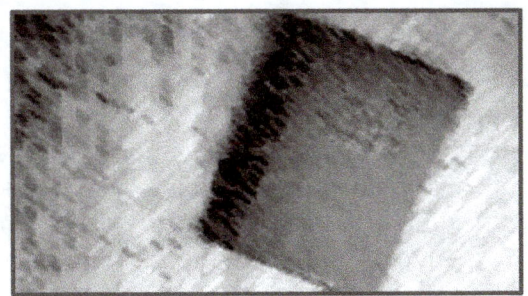

Lesson 12 – God's Useful Book

Memory Verse: *"All Scripture is God-breathed and is useful for teaching, rebuking, correcting and training in righteousness, 17 so that the servant of God may be thoroughly equipped for every good work." 2 Timothy 3:16-17, NIV*

Open in Prayer:

Introduction:

"A Roman Catholic priest in Belgium rebuked a young woman and her brother for reading that 'bad book' pointing to the Bible. 'Mr. Priest,' she replied, 'a little while ago my brother was an idler, a gambler, a drunkard, and made such a noise in the house that no one could stay in it. Since he began to read the Bible, he works with industry, goes no longer to the tavern, no longer touches cards, brings home money to his poor old mother, and our life at home is quiet and delightful. How comes it, Mr. Priest, that a bad book produces such good fruits?'" 1

Read: **2 Timothy 3:14-17**

"But as for you, continue in what you have learned and have become convinced of, because you know those from whom you learned it, 15 and how from infancy you have known the Holy Scriptures, which are able to make you wise for salvation through faith in Christ Jesus. 16 All Scripture is God-breathed and is useful for teaching, rebuking, correcting and training in righteousness, 17 so that the servant of God[a] may be thoroughly equipped for every good work."
(NIV)

Big Idea: *The Bible Came from God's mouth, through the individual writers affirming its useability....*

Going Deeper – Study Guide

The Bible is transformative and can change people for the good.

In fact, it has been said by some to be a divinely fortified book-not just any book- so it can be believed fully. That is probably true for several reasons however, because it's not just some great literary work, like we might see in a university, or a library, or even in a bookstore. We can place our trust in its reliability because it's more of a literary miracle, if anything. There really can't be anything earthly compared with it, because it's not earthly in its origin.

Consider, that a group of individuals didn't sit on a committee and even plan the sixty-six books of the Bible. Rather, more than forty different authors labored for over a span of sixty generations and over three continents. We saw in v. 16 that: *"All Scripture is God-breathed."* Carrying this idea that it came directly from God's mouth and speaking through everyday people of various backgrounds.

1. *What Are Reasons People Might Not Believe the Bible's Reliability?* (Explain) ___
   _____
   _____
   _____

2. *What Practical Areas of Life Can the Bible Be Applied?* (Be Specific)
   a. _____ b. _____
   c. _____ d. _____

   3. *Read the Following Verses and Describe What is Affected by the Scriptures?*

Daniel 9:2:	
Psalm 119:1:	
Matthew 22:29:	
Luke 24:27:	
Acts 17:11:	
Romans 15:4:	

The Bible is also an especially *pertinent* book with uses that lead to spiritual growth because it's not a book that is just useful for something trivial, or something just to pass the

time. It's a book that has a clear, decisive and important function, that's relevant for all things. However, it's especially useful for the matter in the spiritual growth of anyone.

In v.16 it says: *"All Scripture, is God-breathed and is useful for teaching, rebuking, correcting and training in righteousness."*

4. **What Three Aspects of Spiritual Growth is the Bible Pertinent For?**

a. _____ b. _____ c. _____

5. **Explain the Difference Between Reading Your Bible and Studying Your Bible?**
(Explain Your Answers) _____
_____
_____

He lists clear benefits or uses that come from God's word that even though he was telling Timothy about, are for really everyone, regardless of who we are. One version uses the word *"profitable"* which I kind of like, because it's kind of just gets your attention more than *useful*. That we can profit when we read the bible is encouraging to say the least. He also expands in v. 16 when he says: *"Teaching, rebuking, correcting."* All things that are needed at different seasons of a Christ follower's life in many cases.

6. **What is the Benefit of God's Word in the Following Verses?**

Leviticus 25:18:	
Joshua 1:7-8:	
Acts 18:28:	
1 Corinthians 15:3-4:	

Finally, we don't read the Bible not to acquire information or be puffed up with knowledge but that we grow in faith, holiness, and purity. In the last part of v. 16 the Apostle Paul was giving Timothy the final goal of the Bible, *"and training in righteousness."*

Going Deeper – Study Guide

God's ultimate desire for his children is that we all grow in righteousness and apply what we learn. There is probably no book that's more relevant for today's culture, even though it may look different than the culture of the day.

Nobody ever outgrows Scripture; the book widens and deepens with our years. – Charles Spurgeon 2

Challenge:
HOW CAN I DO GOOD TO THOSE AROUND ME? _____   _____   _____   WHAT AREA OF THE BIBLE DO I NEED TO GROW IN? _____   _____   _____   WHAT AREAS HAVE I NOT ALLOWED THE BIBLE TO NOT CHANGE ME? _____   _____   _____   _____

Going Deeper:

Context might clarify the times that were prevalent during the writing of first and second Timothy. There were a lot of different works that were popular, however, written works were not as readily available as today. However, both Jews and Christians were relying heavily on Old Testament Scrolls and the new letters and epistles that were being circulated among the churches. In fact, ***Zondervan Illustrated Bible Backgrounds Commentary of the New Testament*** says:

"The religions of Greece and Rome in Paul's time were not dependent on written materials. There were sacred books containing oracular materials (e.g., the Sibylline Oracles), magic books with spells, incantations, charms, and so forth (cf. Acts 19:19), and other kinds of handbooks on practices such as augury (the interpretation of various omens). Moreover, the writing of the ancient poets like Homer or Hesiod were regarded as having particular authority in their myths about the gods, though at the same time there was a popular saying: 'The poets tell many lies,' especially about the gods. In contrast, both Judaism and its offspring, Christianity, were and are religions that rely heavily on the inspired and authoritative Scriptures." 3

Going Deeper Response

MAKE A PRAYER LIST ABOUT THE TANGIBLE WAYS YOU NEED GOD'S HELP FOR AND COMMIT TO READ YOUR BIBLE 3 SPECIFIC TIMES THIS WEEK

Pray: _Asking God for the desire and wisdom to learn the Scriptures in a greater way and apply them...._

_____

Lesson written by Pastor Frank & Samuel Gervasi

_____

Works Cited:

1. Ministry 127, https://ministry127.com/resources/illustration/the-fruit-of-the-bible/ as accessed on 09/15/2024
2. Deeper Christian Quotes, https://deeperchristian.com/scripture-study-quotes/, as accessed on 04/12/2025.
3. (Zondervan Illustrated Bible Backgrounds Commentary of the New Testament, Copyright © 2002. All rights reserved.

Lesson 13 – Follow Me

Memory Verse: *"And whoever does not carry their cross and follow me cannot be my disciple." Luke 14:27, NIV*

Open in Prayer:

Introduction:

Phillip "Jim" Eliot was an evangelist and Christian missionary who died pursuing his life's ambition of taking the gospel to unreached people. On January 8, 1956, he and four American missionary companions were speared to death on a remote beach by ten men of the primitive Auca/Waorani tribe—the tribe he had felt called to evangelize. Yet Jim Eliot's widow, Elisabeth, held no grudges toward her husband's murderers. Instead, she and several other women moved to the Auca village to continue the work their husbands began. Just one year after the five missionaries were slain in Ecuador, she wrote, "We have proved beyond any doubt that [God] means what He says – His grace is sufficient, nothing can separate us from the love of Christ. We pray that if any, anywhere, are fearing that the cost of discipleship is too great, that they may be given to glimpse that treasure in heaven promised to all who forsake." 1

Read: *Luke 14:25-35*

"Large crowds were traveling with Jesus, and turning to them he said: 26 "If anyone comes to me and does not hate father and mother, wife and children, brothers and sisters—yes, even their own life—such a person cannot be my disciple. 27 And whoever does not carry their cross and follow me cannot be my disciple. 28 "Suppose one of you wants to build a tower. Won't you first sit down and estimate the cost to see if you have enough money to complete it? 29 For if you lay the foundation and are not able to finish it, everyone who sees it will ridicule you, 30 saying, 'This person began to build and wasn't able to finish.' 31 "Or suppose a king is about to go to war against another king. Won't he first sit down and consider whether he is able with ten thousand men to oppose the one coming against him with twenty thousand? 32 If he is not able, he will send a delegation while the other is still a long way off and will ask for terms of peace. 33 In the same way, those of you who do not give up everything you have cannot be my disciples. 34 "Salt is good, but if it loses its

Going Deeper – Study Guide

saltiness, how can it be made salty again? 35 It is fit neither for the soil nor for the manure pile; it is thrown out. 'Whoever has ears to hear, let them hear.'" (NIV)

Big Idea: *Jesus wants every part of our lives, both spiritual and physical, devoted to Him and His kingdom.*

Sometimes the Christian life can demand a lot from the believer. In a spiritual sense, following Jesus can always seem to stretch a person, because everybody brings a different background, character flaws, and ways of doing things that God wants to alter. Even physically, believers may experience sickness and disease that God uses for His glory.

1. *What Habits or Mindsets Do You Feel That You Brought into Your Christian Life?*
   _____
   _____
   _____

2. *What Area Has Been the Hardest to Let Go of or Leave Behind?*

   a. _____ b. _____ c. _____

In our passage today, we can clearly see that Jesus wants first place in our lives for all things. He wants our full allegiance, and the deepest place in our hearts. We see in verse 26: *"If anyone comes to me and does not hate father and mother, wife and children…even their own life – such a person **cannot** be my disciple."* (emphasis added)

3. *What Do the Following Verses Say About Being a Follower?*

Leviticus 20:6:	
Numbers 32:15:	
Judges 2:19:	
2 Kings 18:6:	
Luke 9:57:	
Philippians 3:17:	

Going Deeper – Study Guide

To clarify, Jesus is not saying that people should despise their families looking back in Luke; families are a gift from God (Matthew 15:4; 1 Timothy 5:8).

Rather, Jesus is saying we should be so thoroughly and passionately dedicated to Him, that our love for other things pales in comparison so much, it's like hatred. To be a disciple, you must love Jesus more than those relationships.

4. **What Does Surrender Mean in Your Own Words?** *(Be Specific)* _____

_____

_____

Insight: *We must understand our commitment in walking with Christ, so we aren't discouraged when life gets hard. Because following Jesus is the most important decision a person can make. God wants whole-hearted disciples that are committed to complete surrender.*

5. **What Stands Out in the Following Verses About Yielding?**

Joshua 24:23:	
Psalm 85:12:	
Isaiah 42:8:	
1 Corinthians 7:4:	

Sometimes, that wholehearted allegiance means dying to the old ways of life. Look at verse 27: *"Whoever does not carry their cross and follow me cannot be my disciple."* Think about that – Jesus wants our goals, our plans, and our dreams submitted completely for His use. To be identified with Christ means dying to old ways, old thought patterns, even old relationships if they hinder our walk with the Lord. Finally, look at verse 33: *"In the same way, those of you who do not give up everything you have **cannot be my disciples**."* It doesn't get much clearer than that! Our families, our careers, our desires, even the tangible things we take for granted, belong to God. And when we lay those things at His feet to follow Him, we'll find it was the best place to put them.

"Salvation is free, but discipleship will cost you your life." Dietrich Bonhoeffer 2

Going Deeper – Study Guide

Challenge:

WHAT DOES IT COST ME TO FOLLOW JESUS? _____
_____
_____

WHAT DOES IT MEAN TO BE IDENTIFIED WITH CHRIST? _____
_____
_____

WHAT WAYS HAS FOLLOWING CHRIST MADE ME A BETTER PERSON? _____
_____
_____

Going Deeper:

Verse 34 says, *"Salt is good, but if it loses its saltiness, how can it be made salty again? It is fit neither for the soil nor for the manure pile; it is thrown out."* Regarding this verse, the John MacArthur Study Bible says this: *"Salt was an essential item in first-century Palestine...In a hot climate, without refrigeration, salt was the practical means of preserving food."* **3** In the same way, we should leave others that we encounter wanting to know more about our faith.

Pray: *Close in Prayer for God to help me follow Him, no matter what it costs me*

Going Deeper Response

MAKE A LIST DETAILING THE AREAS WHERE WE FEEL WE NEED TO LEAVE OTHERS WANTING MORE OF CHRIST. THEN COMMIT THOSE AREAS IN PRAYER...

Lesson written by Pastor Frank & Samuel Gervasi

_____

1. Christianity Today, Vol. 1, reprinted Vol. 40, no. 10, https://www.gotquestions.org/Jim-Elliot.html, as accessed on 03/20/2025
2. Dietrich Bonhoffer, The Cost of Discipleship, pg. 39, New York: Macmillan Publishing Company, 1963; first published, 1937.
3. MacArthur Study Bible, Bible Gateway Plus, www.biblrgateway.com, Copyright © John F. MacArthur, published by Thomas Nelson, 2006.

Lesson: 14 – Doing Your Best

Memory Verse: *"Let us not become weary in doing good, for at the proper time we will reap a harvest if we do not give up." Galatians 6:9, NIV*

Open In Prayer:

Introduction:
"It took less than ten seconds for Jamaican sprinter Usain Bolt to cover the one-hundred-meter distance on the Olympic track and win the gold medal in London. Those few seconds cemented his status as the "fastest man alive" and placed him on the winner's podium once again. But the race was not won in those seconds—it was won by hours and hours of practice, workouts, weightlifting, special diet, and coaching. The race was not won in the performance but in the preparation. It is our desire for something greater that causes us to sacrifice some things, even some good things, for the sake of things that are better." 1

Read Galatians 6:1-10

"Brothers and sisters, if someone is caught in a sin, you who live by the Spirit should restore that person gently. But watch yourselves, or you also may be tempted. 2 Carry each other's burdens, and in this way you will fulfill the law of Christ. 3 If anyone thinks they are something when they are not, they deceive themselves. 4 Each one should test their own actions. Then they can take pride in themselves alone, without comparing themselves to someone else, 5 for each one should carry their own load. 6 Nevertheless, the one who receives instruction in the word should share all good things with their instructor. 7 Do not be deceived: God cannot be mocked. A man reaps what he sows. 8 Whoever sows to please their flesh, from the flesh will reap destruction; whoever sows to please the Spirit, from the Spirit will reap eternal life. 9 Let us not become weary in doing good, for at the proper time we will reap a harvest if we do not give up. 10 Therefore, as we have opportunity, let us do good to all people, especially to those who belong to the family of believers." (NIV)

<u>**Big Idea:**</u> *Doing Our Best is God's Will and Will Pay off in the Long Run.*

We may not make the same sacrifices an athlete makes, but we all must lay down a natural human tendency of complacency and pride, and choose to do our best, especially in matters of our faith. The Apostle Paul admonishes us in verse 4 to *"do good to everyone"*, and to *"share each other's burdens, and in this way obey the law of Christ."* V. 2.

These verses aren't saying that believers should follow *Mosaic* Law; rather, he was speaking in a fashion that some in that church understood. Although we are no longer under the Law, it's clear that doing good and living like Jesus (*the "law of Christ"*) is pleasing to the Lord.

1. ***What Are Ways We Can Please Christ in Addition to Doing Good to Others?***
    (Explain our Answers) _____

    _____

    _____

2. ***What Areas Have I Not Been Pleasing to Christ?*** *(Be Specific)* _____

    _____

    _____

Doing good starts with looking at ourselves first. We see in verses 4-5: *"Pay careful attention to your **own** work, for then you will get the satisfaction of a job well done, and then you won't need to compare yourself to anyone else."* (NIV) This is good advice for all of us, because something gets lost when our attention starts focusing on what others should be doing. Although it may be difficult, we need to focus on our walk with Christ if we want to do our best, understanding that *"You are not that important."* v. 3b

3. ***Who Was Being Helped in the Following Verses?***

Judges 21:22:	
Luke 8:3:	
Acts 9:36:	
1 Timothy 5:10:	
Philemon 1:13:	

Going Deeper – Study Guide

Finally, look back at verses 9-10: *"So, let us not become weary in doing what is good. At just the right time we will reap a harvest of blessings if we do not give up. Therefore, whenever we have the opportunity, we should do good to everyone, especially in the family of faith."*
(NIV)

Doing our best will always pay off in due time. We may not see it right away. We may not see it next month, or even next year. But God has promised He will bless those who do their best, in whatever form that blessing He chooses.

4. **What Are Reasons Doing Good to Others Can Be Hard at Times?** *(Explain Your Answers)* _____
_____
_____

5. **Tell me About a Time When Someone Did Good to You?** *(Be Specific)* _____
_____
_____

Insight: *We will reap what we sow in life. Although God often graciously gives us what we don't deserve, it is a natural law of God that the more a person lives to please their flesh, the more death and decay they experience. We cannot live however we want; we must choose to live according to God's Word if we want to do our best and receive our reward.*

Looking back in Galatians, notice that these verses say, ***"we will** reap a harvest".* This phrase sounds definitive in the fact that those who do good will be rewarded by God's own hand. But notice that that harvest only comes *"if we do not give up".* Don't be discouraged if the waiting is getting long; giving our best to God and obeying the law of Christ will be worth it in the end. Stand strong and continue choosing to do good until your harvest comes.

6. **What Do the Following Verses Say About Endurance?**

Romans 15:4:	
2 Corinthians 1:6:	
Colossians 1:11:	
1 Thessalonians 1:3:	
2 Timothy 3:10:	

Challenge:

IN WHAT WAYS CAN I DO GOOD TO THOSE AROUND ME? _____
_____
_____

HOW CAN I GROW IN DOING GOOD? _____
_____
_____

WHAT AREAS NEED IMPROVEMENT? _____
_____
_____

Going Deeper:

Regarding the principle of reaping and sowing, the CSB *Tony Evans Study Bible* says this:

"God has established certain laws that govern the universe he has made. This is true in the physical world (e.g., the law of gravity). But it's true of the spiritual world as well. Paul articulates an important spiritual law or principle when he says, whatever a person sows he will also reap. A farmer harvests exactly what he plants. If he sows potatoes, he won't be looking to harvest green beans. Decide what you want to harvest spiritually and let that control what you decide to sow. This law is universal (it applies to all people everywhere) and inviolable (it proves true without fail). Don't kid yourself into believing that you can rebel against God without consequence." 2

Going Deeper Response

THINK OF 3-4 PEOPLE YOU KNOW AND MAKE A LIST DETAILING THE WAYS YOU CAN DO GOOD TO THEM. THEN MAKE THE TIME TO ACT ON THEM.

Pray: **Asking for God to help me persevere until the harvest comes, giving my best to Him and following His will...**

_____

Lesson written by Pastor Frank & Samuel Gervasi

_____

1. Ministry 127, https://ministry127.com/resources/illustration/the-fastest-man-alive, as accessed on 03/20/2025.
2. Tony Evans Study Bible, Copyright © 2017 by Holman Bible Publishers, Bible Gateway Plus, www.biblegateway.com, as accessed on 03/20/2025.

Going Deeper – Study Guide

Lesson 15 – A Time for Everything

Memory Verse: *"There is a time for everything, and a season for every activity under the heavens..."* **Ecclesiastes 3:1, NIV**

Open in Prayer:

Introduction:
"If you're ever walking the streets of Boston and it starts to rain, look down—you might see something surprising. Boston's City Hall and the nonprofit group Mass Poetry are "slowly bringing secret art to the streets", through a combination of stencils, waterproof spray paint, and rainy days. Since the beginning of April, poems have been sprayed with waterproof paint on sidewalks throughout the city. When the sidewalk is dry, the words are invisible; but when the sidewalk is wet, a piece of art suddenly appears. For many people, a rainy day isn't an ideal day – but who knows what beautiful things a person might miss if it hadn't been for the rain?" 1

In life, seasons come, and seasons go. We cling tightly to some of them and refuse to move on to new ones. In others, we rush to move on as quickly as possible to a more comfortable situation. But we do not have very much say-so when they change. However, we do know that God has power over our seasons in life, regardless of how long they last.

Read: *Ecclesiastes 3:1-14*

"There is a time for everything, and a season for every activity under the heavens: 2 a time to be born and a time to die, a time to plant and a time to uproot, 3 a time to kill and a time to heal, a time to tear down and a time to build, 4 a time to weep and a time to laugh, a time to mourn and a time to dance, 5 a time to scatter stones and a time to gather them, a time to embrace and a time to refrain from embracing, 6 a time to search and a time to give up, a time to keep and a time to throw away, 7 a time to tear and a time to mend, a time to be silent and a time to speak, 8 a time to love and a time to hate, a time for war and a time for peace. 9 What do workers gain from their toil? 10 I have seen the burden God has laid on the human race. 11 He has made everything beautiful in its time.

He has also set eternity in the human heart; yet[a] no one can fathom what God has done from beginning to end. 12 I know that there is nothing better for people than to be happy and to do good while they live. 13 That each of them may eat and drink and find satisfaction in all their toil—this is the gift of God. 14 I know that everything God does will endure forever; nothing can be added to it and nothing taken from it. God does it so that people will fear him." (NIV)

<u>Big Idea:</u> *Every season in life, both good and bad, is sovereignly ordained by God and is needed to receive God's best for us.*

Notice how verse 1 says, *"There is a time for everything, and a season for every activity under the heavens..."* Some versions use the phrase *"appointed times"* (NASB), which implies that someone other than us is doing the appointing. And we know from the rest of Scripture that person is God Himself.

1. Why Can Thinking of Seasons Seem Comforting? *(Explain Your Answers)*

_____

_____

_____

2. How Can We Trust God During Difficult Seasons? *(Be Specific)* _____

_____

_____

Everything that happens to us can be traced back to God's sovereign hand. Absolutely nothing comes into our lives without either God being the originator, or without God allowing it. For some, this can be bad news. If a person is prideful and needs to take credit for the outcome or is uncomfortable trusting God without knowing why He allows the bad seasons, this passage is far from encouraging. But for those of us who choose submission and can rest in the promise that God will *"...cause all things to work together for the good of those who love him,"* (Romans 8:28, NIV) this passage is comforting to hear.

3. Look Up the Following Verses and Highlight What They Show About God's Sovereignty?

2 Samuel 7:20:	
2 Samuel 7:28:	
1 Kings 8:53:	
Psalm 68:20:	
Psalm 140:7:	

Not only are all seasons, good and bad, ordained by God, but they are fully needed as well. Both highs and lows are important for every person; we cannot have one without the other. Verses 2-8 list *"A time for"* twenty-eight common events that many people go through in life. Most often, it's easier to welcome the good events identified in this list, and it's a lot easier to ignore or avoid the rough times. However, God uses both to accomplish His purposes in each person.

4. What Common Events Are Going on in Your Life Where You See God's Hand Working? *(Explain Your Answers)* **a.** _____ **b.** _____

c. _____ **d.** _____

5. If God has appointed every season of our lives, and is using them to accomplish His purposes in us, how are we to respond? *(Explain Your Answers)* _____

_____

_____

We should learn to be content with whatever God has given us. Look again at verses 12-13: *"I know that there is nothing better for people than to be happy and to do good while they live. That each of them may eat and drink and find satisfaction in all their toil—this is the gift of God."* (NIV)

Insight: *Every season in life should cause us to fear God and develop a deep, healthy reverence for Him. Regardless of where we are in life, God is always worthy of our respect, honor, and reverence.*

6. What Do the Following Verses Say About Contentment? *(Be Specific)*

Joshua 7:7:	
Psalm 131:2:	
Proverbs 19:23:	
Luke 3:14:	
1 Timothy 6:6:	
Hebrews 13:5:	

Going Deeper – Study Guide

To clarify, I want to say that looking back in Ecclesiastes, these verses do not imply that we shouldn't aspire to better things in life. Or that we should accept everything that comes our way, even if others are treating us unfairly or unjustly. What it is saying is that we should learn to make the most of our everyday routines that we take for granted sometimes. Philippians 4:12-13 says this: *"I know what it is to be in need, and I know what it is to have plenty. I have learned the secret of being content in any and every situation, whether well fed or hungry, whether living in plenty or in want. I can do all this through him who gives me strength."* (NIV) We should be people who learn to be content with where God has us for that specific reason.

Challenge:
WHAT SEASON OF LIFE AM I IN RIGHT NOW? _____   _____   _____   HOW CAN I LEARN TO FEAR GOD AND BE CONTENT WHERE I AM? _____   _____   _____   WHAT HAS ME CONCERNED ABOUT THIS SEASON OF LIFE RIGHT NOW?   _____   _____   _____

Going Deeper:

Regarding Ecclesiastes 3, the **Jamieson, Fausset, & Brown Bible Commentary** says the following: *"Earthly pursuits are no doubt lawful in their proper time and order (Ecc 3:1-8), but unprofitable when out of time and place; as for instance, when pursued as the solid and chief good (Ecc 3:9, 10); whereas God makes everything beautiful in its season, which man obscurely comprehends (Ecc 3:11). God allows man to enjoy moderately and virtuously His earthly gifts (Ecc 3:12, 13). What consoles us amidst the instability of earthly blessings is, God's counsels are immutable (Ecc 3:14)."* **2**

Going Deeper Challenge
LIST THE LAST 3 SEASONS YOU'VE HAD AND DESCRIBE IN DETAIL HOW GOD WORKED THEM OUT.

Pray: *Thanking God for both the good and tough times He has ordained and asking Him to help me be content….*

Lesson written by Pastor Frank & Samuel Gervasi

1. Preaching Today, https://www.preachingtoday.com/illustrations/2016/may/bostons-secret-street-art.html, as accessed on 03/20/2025.
2. Jamieson, Fausset, & Brown Bible Commentary, 1971, Bible Gateway Plus, www.biblegateway.com, as accessed on 03/20/2025.

Lesson 16 – A King Disgraced

Memory Verse: *"About three in the afternoon Jesus cried out in a loud voice, 'Eli, Eli, lema sebachthani?' (which means 'My God, my God, why have you forsaken me?')" Matthew 27:46, NIV*

Open in Prayer

Introduction:

One of the most infamous personalities of the late nineteenth century was Marie Antoinette, queen of France. While her nation was in economic crisis and her people starving, Marie Antoinette was known for her opulent and luxurious lifestyle. She regularly held balls and banquets at the royal palace and was a generous patron to many composers and musicians. She was an avid gambler, often playing to excess, both losing and winning large sums, to such an extent that the King became worried and banned some of the riskier games that were swallowing up entire fortunes. And it has been rumored that when told that the people of Paris had no bread, Queen Marie responded, "Then let them have cake." 1 This queen knew how to get the most out of her royal position.

While Marie Antoinette represents an extreme, many kings and queens have been known to enjoy the luxuries of royalty, whether that be expensive goods, the praise of their people, or the obedience of their every command. In Matthew 27, we are presented with a King – the King of Kings, in fact. But this King doesn't seem to demand the luxuries of His position. Instead, He bears undeserved abuse and mistreatment at the hands of His subjects to change the course of human history forever.

Going Deeper – Study Guide

Matthew 27:27-50

*"Then the soldiers of the governor took Jesus into the [a]Praetorium and gathered the whole Roman [b]cohort to Him. 28 And they stripped Him and put a red [c]cloak on Him. 29 And after twisting together a crown of thorns, they put it on His head, and put a [d]reed in His right hand; and they knelt down before Him and mocked Him, saying, "Hail, King of the Jews!" 30 And they spit on Him, and took the reed and beat Him on the head. 31 And after they had mocked Him, they took the cloak off Him and put His own garments back on Him, and led Him away to crucify Him. 32 As they were coming out, they found a man of Cyrene named Simon, [e]whom they compelled to carry His [f]cross. 33 And when they came to a place called Golgotha, which means Place of a Skull, 34 they gave Him wine mixed with [g]bile to drink; and after tasting it, He was unwilling to drink it. 35 And when they had crucified Him, they divided His garments among themselves by casting [h]lots. 36 And sitting down, they began to keep watch over Him there. 37 And above His head they put up the charge against Him [i]which read, "THIS IS JESUS THE KING OF THE JEWS." 38 At that time two [j]rebels *were being crucified with Him, one on the right and one on the left. 39 And those passing by were [k]speaking abusively to Him, shaking their heads, 40 and saying, "You who are going to destroy the temple and rebuild it in three days, save Yourself! If You are the Son of God, come down from the cross." 41 In the same way the chief priests also, along with the scribes and elders, were mocking Him and saying, 42 "He saved others; [l]He cannot save Himself! He is the King of Israel; let Him now come down from the cross, and we will believe in Him. 43 He has trusted in God; let God rescue Him now, if He [m]takes pleasure in Him; for He said, 'I am the Son of God.'" 44 And the [n]rebels who had been crucified with Him were also insulting Him in the same way. 45 Now from the [o]sixth hour darkness [p]fell upon all the land until the [q]ninth hour. 46 And about the ninth hour Jesus cried out with a loud voice, saying, "Eli, Eli, lema sabahthani?" that is, "My God, My God, why have You forsaken Me?" 47 And some of those who were standing there, when they heard it, said, "This man is calling for Elijah." 48 And immediately one of them ran, and taking a sponge, he filled it with sour wine and put it on a reed, and gave Him a drink. 49 But the rest of them said, "[r]Let us see if Elijah comes to save Him[s]." 50 And Jesus cried out again with a loud voice and gave up His spirit." (NIV)*

Big Idea: *Christ our King suffered the ridicule of man and the abandonment of the Father that we might receive the forgiveness of God.*

Jesus's kingship is acknowledged in our text – but in the context of mocking and scorn. Initially, the guards mock Him in verses 28-29: *"They stripped him and put a scarlet robe on him and then twisted together a crown of thorns and set it on his head. They put a staff in his right hand. Then they knelt in front of him and mocked him. 'Hail, king of the Jews!' they said."*

Going Deeper – Study Guide

1. **What Thoughts Come to Mind When you Consider What the guards Did to Jesus?** *(Explain Your Answers)* _____

_____

_____

2. **Why Did Jesus Have to go the Cross?** *(Be Specific)* _____

_____

_____

Next, looking back at Matthew, the crowds at His crucifixion join in, as we see in verse 42: *"'He saved others,' they said, 'but he can't save himself! He's the king of Israel! Let him come down from the cross, and we will believe in him.'"* (NIV) Even the sign above Jesus's head – THIS IS JESUS, KING OF THE JEWS – has a tone of mockery in it. Jesus, the King of the Universe, humbled Himself beyond belief for the sake of the very people who ridiculed Him.

3. **What Do the Following Verses Show About the Messiah?**

Jeremiah 23:1:	
Daniel 9:25:	
Matthew 2:4:	
Matthew 16:16:	
John 4:25:	

But out of everything that Jesus endured, the worst was not the rejection of the people, but the rejection of the Father – the One who had sent Him. Verses 45-46 say, *"From noon until three in afternoon darkness came over all the land. About three in the afternoon Jesus cried out in a loud voice, 'Eli, Eli, lema sebachthani?' (which means 'My God, my God, why have you forsaken me?')"* God the Father had to turn His back on Christ, because for that time, the sins of the world were put upon Him. 2 Corinthians 5:21 describes it like this: *"He made Him who knew no sin to be sin on our behalf, so that we might become the righteousness of God in Him."* (NASB)

4. **What Do the following Verses Say About Sin?**

Leviticus 5:13:	
Matthew 5:30:	
Matthew 9:6:	
John 1:29:	

Going Deeper – Study Guide

| **Romans 2:12:** | |
| **2 Corinthians 5:21:** | |

Jesus's ridicule and suffering does end in verse 50: *"And when Jesus had cried out again in a loud voice, he gave up his spirit."* (NIV)

Insight: *Christ our King died a shameful death – crucified as a common criminal. He humbled Himself and took on the judgment we deserved, so that we could be set free.*

Why is this important for us? Because through all this mistreatment Jesus received, and through the offering of His life, death had been conquered! The spotless Lamb, who has taken away the sins of the sins of the world, paid the ultimate price for a lost humanity. Christ made an acceptable sacrifice to cover our sins once and for all, and to reconcile us to God the Father. Because Jesus endured the ridicule of people and the rejection of the Father, He made a way to restore our relationship with God. And that is why He is worthy of being called the King of Kings.

Challenge:
DO I UNDERSTAND AND APPRECIATE WHAT JESUS DID AT THE CROSS? _____   _____   _____   HOW CAN I LIVE IN GRATITUDE TODAY? _____   _____   _____   WHAT AREAS HAVE I NOT EMBRACED THAT I DIED TO? _____   _____   _____

Going Deeper:

Verse 34 tells us that the Roman soldiers offered Jesus wine mixed with gall. Some versions use the word myrrh instead of gall. Myrrh, or gall, was a spice derived from plants native to the Arabian desert and parts of Africa. Wine with myrrh was sometimes given to crucifixion victims to deaden the pain, and the Roman soldiers offered it to Jesus, seemingly out of pity. This occurred to fulfill the prophecy of Psalm 69:21: *"They put gall in my food and gave me vinegar for my thirst."* Verse 35 adds that the soldiers gambled for Jesus' clothes, in fulfillment of the prophecy found in Psalm 22:18: *"They divide my clothes among them and cast lots for my garment."*

Going Deeper Response:

MAKE A LIST OF THE AREASOF YOUR LIFE YOU TAKE FOR GRANTED, THAT CHRIST DIES FOR. THEN OFFER THEM IN PRYAER TO GOD THANK HIM THAT HE ENDURED SO MUCH…..

Pray: ***Thanking God for the humiliation He endured for me to be forgiven...***

———————————

Lesson written by Pastor Frank & Samuel Gervasi

———————————

Works cited:

1.   Adapted from https://en.chateauversailles.fr/discover/history/great-characters/marie antoinette#a-queen-at-the-court, as accessed on 03/20/2025

Going Deeper – Study Guide

Lesson 17 – Benefits of a Thankful/Joyful Spirit

Memory Verse: *"I thank my God every time I remember you. 4 In all my prayers for all of you, I always pray with joy."*
Philippians 1:3-4, NIV

Open in Prayer:

Introduction:

In her book, The Hiding Place, "Corrie Ten Boom relates an incident that taught her to be thankful for things we normally would not be thankful for. She and her sister, Betsy, prisoners of the Nazis, had just been transferred to the worst prison camp they had seen yet, Ravensbrück. Upon entering the barracks, they found them extremely overcrowded and infested with fleas. Their Scripture reading from their smuggled Bible that morning........had reminded them to rejoice always, pray constantly, and give thanks in all circumstances. Betsy told Corrie to stop and thank the Lord for every detail of their new living quarters. Corrie at first flatly refused to give thanks for the fleas, but Betsy persisted. Corrie finally agreed to somehow thank God for even the fleas. During the months spent at that camp, they were surprised to find how openly they could hold Bible study and prayer meetings in their barrack without guard interference. Several months later they learned that the guards would not enter the barracks because of the fleas." 1

Thankfulness produces much in a person's life seeing good even when circumstances don't warrant joyfulness.

Read: ***Philippians 1:3-11***

"I thank my God in all my remembrance of you, 4 always offering prayer with joy in my every prayer for you all, 5 in view of your [a]participation in the gospel from the first day until now. 6 For I am confident of this very thing, that He who began a good work [b]among you will complete it [c]by the day of Christ Jesus. 7 [d]For it is only right for me to feel this way about you all, because I have you in my heart, since both in my [e]imprisonment and in the defense and confirmation of the gospel, you all are [f]partakers of grace with me. 8 For God is my witness, how I long for you all with the [g]affection of Christ Jesus. 9 And this I pray, that your love may overflow still more and more in real knowledge and all discernment, 10 so that you may [h]discover the things that are excellent, that you may be sincere and blameless for the day of Christ; 11 having been filled with the fruit of righteousness which comes through Jesus Christ, for the glory and praise of God." (NIV)

Big Idea: *A Thankful and Joyful Spirit Will Produce Spiritual Fruit and Lead to Wanting the Best in Others.*

A thankful mindset will lead to wanting the best in others-especially those we're close to. Because it reveals something important about a person who is thankful and joyful, that the child of God who's walking in the Spirit and finding their joy in Christ, and that they want to see good things in the life of others. Which is exactly what the Apostle Paul wanted for the church in Philippi. In fact, in vv. 7-8 of today's passage he says, *"It is right for me to feel this way about all of you, since I have you in my heart and, whether I am in chains or defending and confirming the gospel, all of you share in God's grace with me. 8 God can testify how I long for all of you with the affection of Christ Jesus." NIV*

1. Why Does Keeping a Thankful Mindset Seem Like a Challenge at Times? *(Explain Your Answers)* _____
_____
_____

2. Is Being Thankful Just Another way of Just Being Positive? *(Explain)* _____
_____
_____

Going Deeper – Study Guide

I found myself thinking that what the Apostle prayed for the church at Philippi is not really one that is common for the average person. However, for the Apostle Paul and the church at Philippi in Asia, it's understandable.

Because this was said to be a church plant that was ---along with friends of his-- from his second missionary journey. And it was also the first Christian church established in Europe. So, he had a deep connection and affection for them, and he wanted to see the best also.

3. What Stands Out in the Following Verses About Thankfulness?

Leviticus 22:29:	
1 Samuel 2:1:	
1 Chronicles 16:8:	
1 Chronicles 16:34:	
Psalm 7:17:	
Psalm 9:1:	

Insight: *A Joyful and Thankful Spirit Should Produce Fruit in Ourselves but Also Those Around Us*

4. When is it Hardest for People to Be Grateful? *(Be Specific)* _____
_____
_____

5. What Are the Reasons That Everyone Can Find to Be Grateful? *(Be Specific)*

a. _____   b. _____
c. _____   d. _____
e. _____

Additionally, if you look at vv. 9-10 some of the Apostle Paul's desire was being shown because it says: *"And this is my prayer: that your love may abound more and more in knowledge and depth of insight, 10 so that you may be able to discern what is best and may be pure and blameless for the day of Christ."*

Going Deeper – Study Guide

First, was growth in love which is an increasing *"brotherly love"* for each other, and those around them. But not just a little bit, because the idea behind the word is this: "*to exceed a fixed number of measures, to be left over and above a certain number or measure.*"**2** Next, was growth in knowledge.

Love is more than this ooey-gooey, mushy feeling of affection for someone. Love should always be based on truth. The idea here is *love that is correct and precise.*

6. What Do the Following Verses Imply About Gratitude?

Psalm 30:12:	
Psalm 35:18:	
Psalm 69:30:	
Acts 27:35:	
Romans 6:17:	
2 Corinthians 9:15:	

"A spirit of thankfulness is one of the most distinctive marks of a Christian whose heart is attuned to the Lord." Billy Graham 3

Then also the Apostle Paul mentions growth in insight. That the church at Philippi would grow in discernment. Which implies *"perception, not only by the senses but by intellect."* **2** So, basically, that they would grow in love, while using all their senses.

Challenge:

HOW GRATEFUL AM I TODAY FOR THOSE THAT GOD HAS PUT IN MY LIFE?
_____
_____
_____

HOW CAN I PRAY FOR THOSE CLOSE TO ME? _____
_____
_____

HOW CAN I SHOW MY GRATITUDE TO THOSE IN MY LIFE? (BE SPECIFIC)
_____
_____
_____

Going Deeper – Study Guide

Going Deeper:

Joyfulness and Thankfulness are traits and mindsets that can help a person in ways that are unexpected. In fact, the Apostle Paul wrote the letter to the church in Philippi at a time when joy was not normally seen. The Apostle Paul was under house arrest when he wrote this letter. As well as several other letters and epistles known as his Prison Epistles. Embarrassment may have been felt and seen because people in the Roman World viewed incarceration as shameful.

The **Zondervan Cultural Backgrounds Study Bible** notes: *"1:7 'I have you in my heart.' Letters between friends often emphasized that each shared the other's sorrows. Paul's defense and vindication for the gospel would also have relevance for their security (see note on v. 25).' I am in chains.' Most people were ashamed to be associated with anyone chained or in custody of the Roman government. This might be particularly the case in Philippi, which emphasized its close ties with Rome, and where Paul had already been publicly charged with undermining order and the Roman customs of which Philippi was particularly proud (Ac 16:20 – 22)."* **4**

Going Deeper Challenge
WRITE OUT PSALM 100 IN YOUR OWN WORDS AND TURN IT INTO A PERSONAL PRAYER TO GOD....

Pray: *Asking God to help me grow in Thankfulness and Joy...*

_____

Lesson written by Pastor Frank & Samuel Gervasi

_____

Works Cited:

1.   The Hiding Place, Chosen Books, 1971
2.   Interlinear Bible, https://www.biblestudytools.com, as accessed on 10/04/2024)
3.   Goodreads, www.goodreads.com, as accessed on 03/20/2025.
4.   Zondervan Cultural Study Bible, Bible Gateway Plus, www.biblegateway.com, as accessed on 03/20/2025.

Lesson 18 – Word to the Wise

Open in Prayer:

Introduction:

In 2004, a painting by Anna Mary Robertson, better known as Grandma Moses, was brought to the Antiques Roadshow for appraisal. Born before the Civil War, Robertson did not take up painting until late in her life. Her primitive style eventually became extremely popular, and her work commanded a high price. The man who brought the painting to be evaluated had lived nearby and his mother was a friend of Grandma Moses. He said, "She was just a wonderful friend of the family. And she would let my mother buy these paintings, which she thought had relatively little value. I guess my mother did, too. She probably bought eight or ten paintings in all, and my guess would be for perhaps under ten dollars each." 1 The painting that was bought for around $10 was appraised as being worth $60,000!

Sometimes, the things God reveals in His Word to be wisdom seem like foolishness to the world. We value something of great worth as of little worth at all, because God's commands seem extreme, make us uncomfortable, or even defy common sense. But because God is the origin of all wisdom, the wisdom He has revealed in Christ will always prove superior to the wisdom that culture endorses.

Going Deeper – Study Guide

"And when I came to you, brothers and sisters, I did not come as someone superior in [a]speaking ability or [b]wisdom, as I proclaimed to you the [c]testimony of God. 2 For I determined to know nothing among you except Jesus Christ, and Him crucified. 3 I also was with you in weakness and fear, and in great trembling, 4 and my [d]message and my preaching were not in persuasive words of [e]wisdom, but in demonstration of the Spirit and of power, 5 so that your faith would not [f]rest on the [g]wisdom of mankind, but on the power of God. 6 Yet we do speak wisdom among those who are mature; a wisdom, however, not of this age nor of the rulers of this age, who are passing away; 7 but we speak God's wisdom in a mystery, the hidden wisdom which God predestined before the ages to our glory; 8 the wisdom which none of the rulers of this age has understood; for if they had understood it, they would not have crucified the Lord of glory." (NIV)

Big Idea: *Jesus is the center and starting point of wisdom, so we should begin with Him if we want to acquire it.*

Notice from our passage that this wisdom with which the Apostle Paul presented the Gospel to the Corinthians was frowned upon by the wisdom of that time: *"We do, however, speak a message of wisdom among the mature, but not the wisdom of this age or of the rulers of this age who are coming to nothing." (NIV, emphasis added)*

1. **What Would You Consider the Wisdom of this Age?** *(Explain)* _____

_____

_____

2. **What is the Difference of the World's Wisdom and God's Wisdom?** *(Explain Your Answers)* _____

_____

_____

The *"wisdom of this age"* is simply a person's understanding of God without the help of the Holy Spirit. Think about how the human mind is so easily affected by self-deception; it's easy to convince ourselves that some idea or decision is right, only to end up being wrong. Instead, the Apostle Paul relied on the wisdom of God, *"a mystery that has been hidden and that God destined for our glory before time began,"* (v. 7, NIV).

Going Deeper – Study Guide

3. What Do the Following Verses Imply or say About Wisdom?

Deuteronomy 34:9:	
1 Kings 3:28:	
1 Kings 4:29:	
Psalm 51:6:	
Psalm 104:24:	
Psalm 111:10:	

4. What Are Reasons People Can Trust in the Wisdom of Man Rather than the wisdom of God? (Be Specific) a. _____

b. _____ c. _____

Because Christ is the center of true wisdom. Since God is the creator and origin of all good things, including wisdom, we cannot experience the full extent of it without Jesus as our foundation and starting point. The Apostle Paul *"resolved to know nothing...except Jesus Christ and him crucified."* Paul understood that who Christ is and what He taught was all that was needed, and that the wisdom of the world could not compare. And the same is true for us.

Insight: *The work of the Holy Spirit is the wisdom of God, and we can trust how that wisdom is manifested and revealed to us through Him.*

---

5. What Do the Following Verses Further Say About Wisdom?

Proverbs 29:3:	
Ecclesiastes 7:12:	
Isaiah 29:14:	
Jeremiah 9:23:	
Luke 2:52:	
1 Corinthians 1:18:	

Proverbs 1:7 says this: *"The fear of the LORD is the beginning of knowledge, but fools despise wisdom and instruction."* May Jesus be our starting point today.

Going Deeper – Study Guide

Challenge:
WHERE DO I LOOK FOR WISDOM? _____   _____   _____   HOW CAN I GROW IN THE WISDOM OF GOD? _____   _____   _____   WHAT AREAS DO I LACK WISDOM? _____   _____   _____

Going Deeper:

In the **Moody Bible Commentary,** Michael G. Vanlaningham points out how the wisdom found in Christ is available to all who believe in Him: *"Mature (v. 6) refers to all believers, not to a few who are insightful. It is possible that by the word **mature** Paul means "mature or spiritual Christians" as opposed to carnal believers, but there are only two categories of people found in 2:1-14, namely those who are purely secular...and those who are Christians (see the many first-person pronouns and verbs found [in the passage] here). In addition, it is highly unlikely that Paul would withhold spiritual truths related to Christ from immature believers. **Mature** here is the term he used for the category of all those who believe in Jesus Christ vis-à-vis the world." 2*

Going Deeper Challenge
WRITE DOWN THE LAST DECISION YOU MADE. RATE IT 1 TO 10 TO SEE IF IT WAS WISE OR NOT? DESCRIBE IT COULD HAVE BEEN IMPROVED OR WISER....

Pray: *Asking God to help me make Him my starting point for wisdom, and choosing to obey Him even when I don't understand...*

_____

Lesson written by Pastor Frank & Samuel Gervasi

_____

1.   Antiques Road Show, https://www.pbs.org/show/antiques-roadshow, as accessed on 03/20/2025.
2.   Moody Bible Commentary, Moody Publishers, Chicago, 2014

Lesson: 19 – Biblical Household Submission

Memory Verse: *"Submit to one another out of reverence for Christ."* **Ephesians 5:21, NIV**

Open in Prayer:

Introduction:

Seatbelts can be a hassle. Some people just don't want to be bothered even when the law requires them to buckle up. According to the Associated Press, a New Zealander named Ivan Segedin took it to an extreme. "The police ticketed him 32 times over five years for failing to use his seat belt. Even though this was costing him a lot of money, Segedin refused to buckle up. Finally, instead of obeying the law, the man decided to rely on deception. He made a fake seat belt that would hang over his shoulder and made it appear that he was wearing a seat belt when he was not. His trick worked for a while. Then, he had a head-on collision. He was thrown forward onto the steering wheel and killed." 1

The choices we make can have serious consequences. God has spelled out standards for the structures of families in the Bible also to assure minimal problems.

Read: *Ephesians 5:21-6:4*

"Submit to one another out of reverence for Christ. 22 Wives, submit yourselves to your own husbands as you do to the Lord. 23 For the husband is the head of the wife as Christ is the head of the church, his body, of which he is the Savior. 24 Now as the church submits to Christ, so also wives should submit to their husbands in everything. 25 Husbands, love your wives, just as Christ loved the church and gave himself up for her 26 to make her holy, cleansing[a] her by the washing with water through the word, 27 and to present her to himself as a radiant church, without stain or

wrinkle or any other blemish, but holy and blameless. 28 In this same way, husbands ought to love their wives as their own bodies. He who loves his wife loves himself.

29 After all, no one ever hated their own body, but they feed and care for their body, just as Christ does the church— 30 for we are members of his body. 31 "For this reason a man will leave his father and mother and be united to his wife, and the two will become one flesh."[b] 32 This is a profound mystery—but I am talking about Christ and the church. 33 However, each one of you also must love his wife as he loves himself, and the wife must respect her husband. 6 Children, obey your parents in the Lord, for this is right. 2 "Honor your father and mother"—which is the first commandment with a promise— 3 "so that it may go well with you and that you may enjoy long life on the earth." [c] 4 Fathers, [d] do not exasperate your children; instead, bring them up in the training and instruction of the Lord." (NIV)

Big Idea: *Families Have Responsibility to Each Other Member of that Household*

All families will have this important characteristic, evident in their structure. Especially, if they are to be successful, and bring forth fruit, that's consistent with God's plan for them. If each person in a family does not grasp this structure, it won't have a sound foundation to stand on or be successful.

1. What Could Be Some Reasons that God Places a High Priority on Families? *(Explain Your Answers)* _____

_____

_____

2. What Are Ways That Our Culture Tries to Re-Define Families Today? *(Be Specific)*

_____

_____

_____

In today's passage the Apostle Paul, in his letter to the church at Ephesus, was giving biblical standards for Christian households.

In v. 21 he says: *"Submit to one another out of reverence for Christ."* Giving us a two-part standard that is important. First, this is the idea of submission. And from a grammatical standpoint, it means literally to: *"arrange under, to subordinate."* However, it's also used as a Greek military term meaning: *"to arrange [troop divisions] in a military fashion under the command of a leader."* **2**

Going Deeper – Study Guide

3. What Do the Following Verses Show About Families?

Genesis 7:1:	
Joshua 2:12:	
2 Kings 8:27:	
1 Chronicles 16:43:	
Proverbs 27:10:	

Additionally, looking back in Ephesians, we see submission had a third usage in non-military way: *"a voluntary attitude of giving in, cooperating, assuming responsibility, and carrying a burden."* **2** So, in essence the Apostle Paul was implying that families were biblically structured in that way. With each having clearly defined roles and expectations in a particular order.

4. What Are Reasons Families Can Be Divided? *(Be Specific)*

a. _____ b. _____ c. _____

5. What Can Be the Downsides of Not Putting God at the Center of a Family? *(Explain)*

_____

_____

Insight: *A Christian Family Ultimately Has a Responsibility Before Christ. Himself.*

---

6. What Do the Following Verses Show About Family Responsibility?

Acts 10:2:	
Joshua 2:12:	
2 Kings 8:27:	
1 Chronicles 16:43:	
Proverbs 27:10:	

In addition to that aspect of submission though, the second aspect that is really rooted in the why we're supposed to submit to one another. And that is because of Christ Himself! If we look at the second part of v. 21, he says: *"Out of reverence for Christ."* With part of that, acknowledging that Christ is giving us the best way to live successfully as families. Following the patterns set forth in the Bible, including this passage today.

What is the Biggest Obstacle Facing the Family Right Now? It is Over-Commitment, Time Pressure. There is Nothing that Will Destroy Family Life More Insidiously than Hectic Schedules and Busy Lives, where Spouses are Too Exhausted to Communicate, Too Worn Out to Have Sex, Too Fatigued to Talk to the Kids. (James Dobson) **3**

Challenge
HOW CAN A FAMILY FUNCTION PROPERLY IF EVERYONE HAS DIFFERENT GOALS AND ARE MOVING IN DIFFERENT DIRECTIONS?_____   _____   _____   HOW CAN WE BE THE BEST FAMILY MEMBER WHERE GOD HAS PLACED US?   _____   _____   _____   AM I SUBMITTING IN REVERENCE OF CHRIST? _____   _____   _____

Going Deeper:

Whatever our role is in the family, we should understand submission and yield to each other for its smooth functioning. The **NKJV Wiersbe Study Bible** says: *"It is only through the power of the Holy Spirit that we can walk in harmony.....the unity of the people of God that Paul described (4:1–16) must be translated into daily living if we are to enjoy the harmony that is a foretaste of heaven on earth. If our homes are to be a heaven on earth, then we must be controlled by the Holy Spirit."* **4**

Going Deeper Challenge
SIT DOWN WITH YOUR FAMILY AND WRITE OUT THE DIFFERENT ROLES IN YOUR CURRENT STRUCTURE AND THEN WRITE WHAT YOU COULD DO BETTER

Pray Asking God to Help You Be the Best Family Member You Could Be......

_____

Lesson written by Pastor Frank & Samuel Gervasi

_____

<u>Works Cited:</u>

1. https://www.sermoncentral.comhttps//www.sermoncentral.com/sermon-illustrations/70702/fake-seatbelts-and-submission-by-sermon-central, as accessed on 10/13/2024)
2. Interlinear Bible, biblestudytools.com, as accessed on 03/20/2025.
3. James Dobson Quotes, https://www.azquotes.com/author/4018-James_Dobson#google_vignette, as accessed on 04/17/2025.
4. NKJV Wiersbe Bible, Copyright 2021, Thomas Nelson.

Lesson 20 – Letting Go

"Wives, submit to your husbands as you do the Lord." **Ephesians 5:22, NIV**

Open in Prayer:

Introduction

"According to the Associated Press, on December 14, 1996, a 763-foot grain freighter was heading down the Mississippi at New Orleans, Louisiana, when it lost control, veered toward the shore, and crashed into a riverside shopping mall. At the time the Riverwalk Mall was crowded with some 1,000 shoppers, and 116 [of those] people were injured [in the freighter's wreck]. After investigating the accident for a year, the Coast Guard reported that the freighter had lost control because the engine had shut down. The engine had shut down because of low oil pressure. The oil pressure was low because of a clogged oil filter. And the oil filter was clogged because the ship's crew had failed to maintain the engine properly." 1

Sometimes, if something is managed and run in a way it wasn't designed to be, the smallest mistakes can have disastrous consequences. The same rings true for the marriage relationship.

Read: *Ephesians 5:22-24*

"Wives, submit yourselves to your own husbands as you do to the Lord. 23 For the husband is the head of the wife as Christ is the head of the church, his body, of which he is the Savior. 24 Now as the church submits to Christ, so also wives should submit to their husbands in everything." (NIV)

Big Idea: Wives have a responsibility in accordance with God's structure for the family to submit to their husbands' leadership.

Going Deeper – Study Guide

1. What Comes to Mind for You When You Hear the Word "Submit"? (Explain)

_____

_____

_____

Verses like the kind we read today have become taboo in modern culture. And to an extent, it's easy to see why. This passage has given birth to wrong teaching, selfish desires for control, and resistance to the principles at hand. However, just because this passage has been misunderstood, does not cancel out or nullify God's roles for the Christian household.

Perhaps the qualifier in verse 22 – *"as you do in the Lord"* – helps us understand submission as God intended it.

2. What Are Different Ways We Submit to Christ?

a. _____

b. _____

c. _____

When we submit to Christ, He doesn't take advantage of us. He doesn't treat us like an insignificant nobody. He doesn't treat us as His slaves. Rather, we are of infinite value to God, and the purpose of Jesus' life, ministry, and death was *"...for **freedom** that Christ has set you free."* (Gal. 5:1, NIV; emphasis added)

3. What Do the Following Verses Say About Jesus' Care as We Submit:

Psalm 95:7:	
Isaiah 40:11:	
Matthew 11:29:	
John 10:10:	

4. In Your Opinion, How Extensive Should Submission Be? *(Explain your Answer)*

_____

_____

_____

So, then, we know what biblical submission is *not*. So, what *is* biblical submission? Biblical submission that honor God is the wife viewing the husband as responsible and acting accordingly. In the end, each husband and father will give account for the kind of stewards they were with their families on earth.

5. How Might Submission Be Related to Worship?

_____

_____

_____

Husbands should be leading in a way that saves and redeems their families and values them as second only to God Himself. And the wife should strengthen her husband in fulfilling that role, not working against him, and striving to submit in a way that supports her husband and glorifies Jesus.

6. What Do the Following Verses Show About Submission?

Job 22:21:	
Proverbs 3:5-6:	
Philippians 2:3-4:	
1 Peter 3:5-6:	

"Submission is the willingness to give up our right to ourselves, to freely surrender our insistence on having our own way all the time." Myles Munroe2

Challenge

What is the family role God has for me?

_____

_____

_____

On a scale of 1 to 10, how often do I submit in a God-honoring way? (1 being the lowest, 10 the highest)

1 – ----------------2.5------------------ 5 --------------------7.5------------------10

How can I grow in fulfilling my God-given role in the family? _____

_____

_____

Going Deeper:

The Dictionary of Bible Themes defines the word submission as follows:

"[Submission is] a humble attitude where obedience is rendered within a relationship; whether it be to God, authorities or other people at work, in the church, in marriage or in the family." **3**

Going Deeper Response

USE A BIBLE CONCORDANCE OR BIBLE DICTIONARY AND LOOK UP THE WORD SUBMISSION FOR STUDY

Pray: Asking God to help me submit and trust His sovereignty in the direction of my family...

_____

Lesson written by Pastor Frank & Samuel Gervasi

_____

1. Taken from *https://sermoncentral.com/sermon-illustrations/9589/losing-control-one-mistake-at-a-time-by-john-williams-iii*, as accessed on 3/20/2025.
2. Quote by Myles Munroe, https://www.goodreads.com/quotes/1245817-submission-is-the-willingness-to-give-up-our-right-to#:~:text=Submission%20is%20the%20willingness%20to%20give%20up%20our%20right%20to,own%20way%20all%20the%20time., as accessed on 04/17/2025.
3. *Dictionary of Bible Themes*, BibleGateway Plus, *www.biblegateway.com*, as accessed on 3/20/2025.
4. New International Bible, Holy Bible, New International Version®, NIV® Copyright ©1973, 1978, 1984, 2011 by Biblica, Inc.® Used by permission. All rights reserved worldwide.

Going Deeper – Study Guide

Lesson 21 – Husbands Leading in Love

Memory Verse: *"Husbands.. love your wives, just as Christ loved the church and gave himself up for her."* **Ephesians 5:25, NIV**

Open in Prayer:

Introduction

The idea that we have the ideal spouse has proved popular in our culture. One source said, *"Among young adults in the U.S. a 2011 poll found that 73% of Americans believed in a soulmate, the idea that 'two people are destined to be together', with fully 80% of those under 30 taking this view. However, for those seeking a soulmate, what matters is emotional skills and the ability to spark romantic or sexual chemistry. These qualities are supposed to put men and women on the path to what they see as the primary goods of marriage: intimacy, self-expression, and self-fulfillment."*[1]

Which may be true with many variables that may make the ideal marriage. Nevertheless, God has spelled out a husband's role, clearly giving him guidelines to follow to fulfill his designed role in the family unit.

Read: *Ephesians 5:25-33*

"Husbands, love your wives, just as Christ loved the church and gave himself up for her 26 to make her holy, cleansing her by the washing with water through the word, 27 and to present her to himself as a radiant church, without stain or wrinkle or any other blemish, but holy and blameless. 28 In this same way, husbands ought to love their wives as their own bodies. He who loves his wife loves himself. 29 After all, no one ever hated their own body, but they feed and care for their body, just as Christ does the church— 30 for we are members of his body. 31 'For this reason a man will leave his father and mother and be united to his wife, and the two will become one flesh.' 32 This is a profound mystery—but I am talking about Christ and the church. 33 However, each one of you also must love his wife as he loves himself, and the wife must respect her husband." (NIV)

Going Deeper – Study Guide

Big Idea: Husbands Have a Responsibility to Their Wives, Treating Them with Care and Respect.

1. What Comes to Mind for You When You Hear the Word "Love"? (Explain)

_____

_____

_____

In today's devotion continuing in our family focus, we discover a husband's role. In Ephesians 5, where the Apostle Paul gives further instructions to families, he addresses the husband. The husband's role is all about *responsibility* – a strong word that gives an image of commitment and being deliberate.

2. What Is the Biggest Thing You've Ever Been Responsible For, and How Did You Handle It?

_____

_____

That commitment and deliberateness manifests itself in favorable and dignified treatment of our spouses. The Apostle Paul is not talking about perfection, or saying that couples don't have their differences, but in the end the treatment is one of respect.

In verses 25-27, he says: *"For husbands, this means love your wives, just as Christ loved the church. He gave up his life for her 26 to make her holy and clean, washed by the cleansing of God's word. 27 He did this to present her to himself as a glorious church without a spot or wrinkle or any other blemish. Instead, she will be holy and without fault."* (NLT)

3. What Do the Following Verses Say About Sacrificial Love:

John 15:13:	
Romans 12:9-10:	
1 John 3:16:	
1 Jonh 4:11:	

Consider how Paul gives us three different examples of what a husband's love for his wife might involve. First, a *sacrificial love*, and one that honors their spouse, with a deep and reverent respect for her. Probably the opposite of what is sometimes seen in our culture. I want to tell you that it irks me when I see people speak about their wives in a negative tone, sharing demeaning things about them with coworkers.

Going Deeper – Study Guide

I've heard people talk about their wives in a disrespectful manner, and I've thought, *what are you doing?* It is rude, plus counter-productive to anything good in that marriage relationship. Think about the comparison used of Christ's love for the church, making her *"holy, spotless, and blameless"* (v. 26.)

4. What Are Some Things a Person May Need to Sacrifice Out of Love for Their Spouse?

a. _____

b. _____

c. _____

Additionally, the Apostle Paul talks about a *respectful love*, because in v. 28, the Bible is saying it's ok to love yourself! *"In this same way, husbands ought to love their wives as their own bodies. He who loves his wife loves himself. After all, no one ever hated their own body, but they feed it and care for their body."*

Insight: Husbands Should Be Loving Their Wives with a Sacrificial, Respectful, and Unified Love.

Even though the words invoke selfish motivation, it's really one of stewardship and taking care of oneself. And, if we're honest we all know how to care for and respect our own bodies. So, it kind of puts things in perspective, doesn't it?

5. What Are Some Practical Ways A Husband Could Show Respectful Love to His Wife? (Be Specific)

_____

_____

_____

Finally, a *unified love* is one that is working together with your spouse, and you're both moving the family in the direction that is best for your family. Because in verse 31 he says, *"'For this reason a man will leave his father and mother and be united to his wife, and the two will become one flesh.'"*

This verse is cross-referencing Genesis 2:24, in which God was ordaining marriage in the first place. And it implies something important – not what is best for your mother or father, or what they would do. It is *your* family, and it should be shaped for you both to work. However, that's not to say that you don't have anything to do with them, or parents can't give some valuable insights. Especially since they know their kids and what might help. But ultimately living your own lives, as husband and wife.

6. What Do the Following Verses Show About a Unified Marriage?

Psalm 133:1:	
Ecclesiastes 4:9-12:	
Amos 3:3:	
Matthew 19:4-6:	

""If you are married, or single hoping to marry, remember this: every marriage is comprised of two sinners. The best marriage is one where those sinners are united in their love of God, their commitment to serve one another, and a spirit of humility. Through marriage you can expect to learn how much sacrifice is involved in loving a sinner through all the ups and downs of life; this is a picture of how Christ loves us." - Kerry van der Vinne 2

Challenge Section

Am I loving my wife the way Christ did the church?

_____

_____

_____

Is my love for her sacrificial or selfish? Respectful or harsh? Unified or divided?

_____

_____

How can I love my wife the way Christ loved me today? _____

_____

_____

Going Deeper:

The **NKJV Maxwell Study Bible** defines the phrase *leadership in the* home as follows: *"Contrary to what many teach, leadership in the home is not about power or control. Paul ask for mutual submission (Eph. 5:21) and calls husbands to be Christ-figures (5:23-25). And how did Christ lead the church? He provided, taught, wept, healed, and died on a cross. Spiritual leadership means giving up yourself for someone else (5:25). It means assuming responsibility for the health and development."* 3

Going Deeper Response

USE A BIBLE CONCORDANCE OR BIBLE DICTIONARY AND LOOK UP THE WORD SUBMISSION FOR STUDY

Pray: Asking God to help me show a sacrificial, respectful, and unified love to my wife...

_____

Lesson written by Pastor Frank & Samuel Gervasi

_____

Works Cited:

1. Adapted from *https://www.preachingtoday.com/illustrations/2024/october/myth-of-perfect-soulmate.html*, as accessed on 10/20/2024.

2. Quote by Kerry van der Vinne, *https://egbella.com/2023/04/02/10-christian-quotes-about-marriage/*, as accessed on 04/17/2025.

3. *NKJV Maxwell Leadership Bible.* Copyright © 2002, 2007, 2018 by Maxwell Motivation, Inc., BibleGateway Plus, *www.biblegateway.com*, as accessed on 3/20/2025.

Lesson 22 – The Children's Part

Memory Verse: *"Children, obey your parents in the Lord, for this is right."*
Ephesians 6:1, NIV

Open in Prayer:

Introduction

Every year, between January 29th and April 15th, people begin the tedious work of filing their taxes. One central component of tax season is claiming exemptions from certain charges. And some of the things people have tried to claim as tax exemptions over the year can be comical from our vantage point. *"For example, one man tried to soften the blow of paying for his daughter's wedding by inviting a few of his businesses clients and writing the wedding off as business entertainment. Others, on more than one occasion, have tried to write off their dog or cat as a dependent. Furthermore, one family constructed a doomsday fallout shelter near their home and tried to claim it as preventative medicine. Obviously, all these claims were denied."* 1

In previous weeks, we have discussed the family roles of both wives and husbands. But some of us are neither. Such people may try to *exempt* themselves from the guidelines given in Ephesians 5-6, like a tax exemption. But while all of us are husbands or wives, we are all somebody's children. And, therefore, we have a role given by God to honor Him in our families.

Read: *Ephesians 6:1-4*

"Children, obey your parents in the Lord, for this is right. 2 'Honor your father and mother'—which is the first commandment with a promise— 3 'so that it may go well with you and that you may enjoy long life on the earth.' 4 Fathers, do not exasperate your children; instead, bring them up in the training and instruction of the Lord." (NIV)

Big Idea: *Children Have a Responsibility to Obey Their Parents if They Want God's Blessing.*

---

1. What Was A Rule Your Family Had Growing Up You Had the Hardest Time Obeying?
(Be Specific)

_____

_____

_____

In our passage today, the Apostle Paul addresses the children at Ephesus and their role in a Christian family structure. Verses 1-3 tell us: *"Children, obey your parents in the Lord, for this is right. 2 'Honor your father and mother'—which is the first commandment with a promise— 3 'so that it may go well with you and that you may enjoy long life on the earth.'"*

2. What Is the Difference Between Obeying Our Parents, and Honoring Our Parents?

    a. _____

    b. _____

    c. _____

Now, it would be easy to note the phrase *"Obey...in the Lord"* (v. 1) and attempt to claim another exemption. Not all of us have parents who are "in the Lord". Some of us have parents that do not know God or follow His Word, or else were flawed in their parenting style.

It's important to remember that all parents are ordained by God and were chosen by Him to raise us. No one gets to choose their families of origin – that role is reserved for God alone, and He does not make mistakes. We should obey our parents regardless of what their relationship to God is, because they are older and wiser than we are. They were sovereignly hand-picked by God to mold us into who He wanted us to become.

3. What Do the Following Verses Say About God's Sovereignty in Choosing Our Parents:

Job 42:2:	
Proverbs 16:33:	
Acts 17:26:	
Romans 8:28:	

4. Why Might We Have a Hard Time Obeying and Honoring Our Parents?

_____

_____

_____

Finally, look back at the promise we're given in verse 2 if we obey: *"'...it may go well with you and that you might enjoy a long life on earth.'"* This verse (which is actually a reference to Exodus 20:12) shows us that this is a cause-and-effect relationship. If we submit to God's

Insight: A person doesn't outgrow obeying his parents when he becomes an adult. All of us, no matter our age, are still called to treat our parents with respect, listen to their advice, and so long as it lines up with Scripture, apply it to our lives.

Word and accept our God-given role in the family, we will get the best results.

5. What Might the Benefits Be of Obeying and Honoring Our Parents? *(Be Specific)*

_____
_____
_____

Whatever role God has given us in the household; we can rest assured that God has a structure and a model for how to glorify Him in that role. And it will always be the best way!

6. What Do the Following Verses Show About Obeying Our Parents?

Deuteronomy 5:16:	
Proverbs 13:1:	
Colossians 3:20:	
2 Timothy 3:1-2:	

"The child that never learns to obey his parents in the home will not obey God or man out of the home." – Susanna Wesley 2

Going Deeper – Study Guide

*What is the family role God has for me?*_____
_____
_____

*How can I grow in fulfilling that role?*_____
_____
_____

*How can I respect and honor my parents today?*_____
_____
_____

Going Deeper:

In conclusion of our four-lesson focus on biblical family roles, the **NIV Biblical Theology Study Bible** notes the importance of Christ being the center of our families, and provides the key to applying these verses to our lives: *"After instructing believers how to live worthy of their calling within the community of faith (4:17—5:20), Paul instructs them how to live within the household. The link between these two sections is 5:21; the submission called for in the household instructions depends on being "filled with the Spirit" (5:18; see note there). These instructions primarily differ from traditional Greco-Roman codes by presenting Christ as the true head of the family. The order within these codes reflects how the Christian household should work out Christ's unity over all things (1:10)."* **3**

Going Deeper Response

USE A BIBLE AND LOOK UP COLOSSIANS 3:18-25. LIST 3 WAYS THEY ARE SIMILAR AND 3 WAYS THEY'RE DIFFERENT.....

Pray: Asking God to help me respect and obey my parents...
_____

Lesson written by Pastor Frank & Samuel Gervasi
_____

1. Adapted from *https://www.turbotax.intuit.com/tax-tips/fun-facts/7-of-the-craziest-illegal-tax-deductions-ever-claimed/L3ZElWEFZ,* as accessed on 3/20/2025.
2. Quote by Susanna Wesley, *https://quotefancy.com/quote/1613728/Susanna-Wesley-The-child-that-never-learns-to-obey-his-parents-in-the-home-will-not-obey,* as accessed on 04/19/2025.
3. *NIV Biblical Theology Study Bible.* Copyright © 2019 by Zondervan, BibleGateway Plus, *www.biblegateway.com,* as accessed on 3/20/2025.
4. New International Bible, Holy Bible, New International Version®, NIV® Copyright ©1973, 1978, 1984, 2011 by Biblica, Inc.® Used by permission. All rights reserved worldwide.

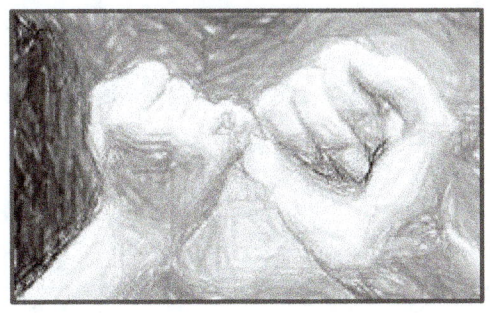

Lesson 23 – I Promise #1

Memory Verse: *"I am with you and will watch over you wherever you go, and I will bring you back to this land. I will not leave you until I have done what I have promised you."* **Genesis 28:15, NIV**

Open in Prayer:

Introduction

"One stormy night an elderly couple entered the lobby of a small hotel and asked for a room. The clerk said they were full, and they would probably find so were all the hotels in town. 'But I can't send a fine couple like you out in the rain. Would you be willing to sleep in my room?' The couple hesitated, but the clerk insisted.

The next morning when the man paid his bill, he said, 'You're the kind of man who should be managing the best hotel in the United States. Someday I'll build you one.' The clerk smiled politely. A few years later the clerk received a letter containing an airplane ticket; the letter invited him to visit New York. When the clerk arrived, his host took him to the corner of 5th Avenue and 34th Street, where there stood a magnificent new building. 'That,' explained the man, 'is the hotel I have built for you to manage.'" The elderly man had not forgotten the promise he had given to the clerk. *"The name of the clerk was William Waldorf Astor, and the hotel was the original Waldorf-Astoria."* 1

In today's lesson, we will begin studying the life of the patriarch Jacob, from the Old Testament book of Genesis. And as we do, we will begin looking at the promises of God.

Read: _Genesis 28:11-15_

"When he reached a certain place, he stopped for the night because the sun had set. Taking one of the stones there, he put it under his head and lay down to sleep. 12 He had a dream in which he saw a stairway resting on the earth, with its top reaching to heaven, and the angels of God were ascending and descending on it. 13 There above it stood the Lord, and he said: 'I am the Lord, the God of your father Abraham and the God of Isaac. I will give you and your descendants the land on which you are lying. 14 Your descendants will be like the dust of the earth, and you will spread out

Going Deeper – Study Guide

to the west and to the east, to the north and to the south. All peoples on earth will be blessed through you and your offspring. 15 I am with you and will watch over you wherever you go, and I will bring you back to this land. I will not leave you until I have done what I have promised you.'"
(NIV)

<u>*Big Idea:*</u> *God has to make the promise first before we can claim it as our own.*

---

1. What Are Some Promises People Commonly Make in Everyday Life? *(Be Specific)*

_____
_____
_____

In our passage today, we see an important promise from God, given specifically to Jacob and his descendants. Nevertheless, God makes promises to his children often in life. However, a person can't always just claim every promise made in Scripture to our own situation. Even though people do it often, it's not necessarily a good thing. Because some are specific to a group or an individual in Scripture most often, even though we may have common things we can apply.

2. What Are Some Promises That Apply to Us as Believers?

a. _____
b. _____
c. _____

In today's reading, the encounter and promise was for Jacob, while he was on his journey. We know from the text that he stops for the night after growing tired. And then we see in v. 11 *"...that he picks up a stone to lay his head on."* Which may not have been the most comfortable surroundings. However, don't forget that Jacob fled in haste. It sometimes seems like God chooses the times when we are most receptive to listen.

3. During Which Seasons of Life Do You Find Yourself Most Receptive to God's Leading?

_____
_____
_____

Also, Jacob encounters God in a dream that was to change his life from that point forward. In v. 12 it says: *"He had a dream in which he saw a stairway resting on the Earth, with its top reaching to heaven. And the angels of God were ascending and descending on it."*

Going Deeper – Study Guide

In this passage, we should look at some background information that can help us. Because what was going on is that Jacob had just fled his home, and run to get away from his brother Esau, in fear for his life.

If you know the story Jacob had done some dishonest and deceitful things in life. In fact, he was called the *Deceiver* (Genesis 25:26) which was characteristic of his nature at that time. Because he had deceived his brother Esau and father Isaac for some important things – namely two: Esau's birthright, and Isaac's blessing. These two things were reserved for the older son and not the youngest (Genesis 25:28-34). Now the birthright was taken over a bowl of stew that Esau wanted and gave it up willingly to Jacob, after returning from hunting all day. And the blessing from Isaac was taken by pretending to be Esau and tricking their elderly father whose sight had gone bad (Genesis 27). And, when Esau finds out what happened, he was upset and Jacob flees to Haran to live with an uncle, which brings us to our current story.

4. What Do the Following Verses Say About Promises:

Genesis 9:11:	
Joshua 9:15:	
2 Samuel 7:28:	
Acts 13:32:	
2 Corinthians 7:1:	

Insight: *If God has made us a promise, we should apply it to our lives the best we can...*

God makes a powerful promise to Jacob, doesn't He? *"I am the LORD, the God of your father Abraham and the God of Isaac."* The same promises that he made earlier to both individuals Abraham and Isaac. And he was reaffirming it again here. And the promise itself was reserved for their descendants because it was a promise for specific land that is still disputed to this day.

Finally, God will do whatever it takes to get our attention in life. Maybe, for some major decision that we are on the brink of making. Maybe, it's about a new job that you've been seeking Him about, or a relationship you find yourself in and don't know how to proceed with it. If that's your goal in the first place. Or maybe it's about a new area of change, and He really wants to get your attention.

117 | P a g e

Going Deeper – Study Guide

5. When Do We Most Need to Be Reminded of God's Promises? *(Be Specific)*

_____

_____

_____

Whatever God promises He will make sure it happens. And it is contingent on God seeing it through, not us.

6. What Do the Following Verses Show About God's Faithfulness?

Joshua 23:14:	
Luke 1:37:	
2 Corinthians 1:20:	
Hebrews 10:23:	

"God will always stay with us and keep all His promises to us, even when we go through the storms of life. When we wonder if He's there, He is!" – Charles Stanley 2

Challenge Section

*What is the promise God has for me?*_____

_____

_____

How can I best apply it to my situation? _____

_____

_____

How can I have confidence that God will be faithful to fulfill it? _____

_____

_____

Going Deeper:

The **NIV Grace & Truth Study Bible** regarding Genesis 28:10-17:

"The author backtracks to describe a particular stopover on Jacob's journey from Beersheba to Harran. About two to three days into his journey, Jacob stops at a place called Luz, located about 60 miles from Beersheba. Ironically, the first time Jacob will truly wake up is when he goes to sleep, for it is in the quietness of inactivity that he hears God. This is the second dream in the Bible in which someone explicitly experiences a revelation from God (cf. 20:3). Jacob dreams of a stairway to heaven on which angels descend and ascend, taking their directions from the Lord, who stands at the top of the staircase. The stairway is more like a ramp than a ladder, resembling the tower of Babel structure, which rebellious humans constructed to unite heaven to earth. In an act of grace, God himself gives the Abrahamic promise directly to Jacob. God now for the first time calls himself not only the God of Abraham but also the God of Isaac. Despite everything, he will also be Jacob's God. When Jacob awakens, awe overwhelms him. The words translated "afraid" and 'awesome' (28:17) come from the same Hebrew word meaning fear. Together they capture the awe-inspiring experience of a creature coming into the presence of its Creator. Jacob responds that this place is significant because it is none other than the house of God ('Bethel') and the gateway of heaven, the place where heaven and earth are united. Jesus will eventually serve as such a bridge between heaven and earth (Jn 1:51), finally bringing the Bible's storyline into complete unity (Rev 21:3)." **3**

Going Deeper Response
USE A BIBLE MAP AND FIND THESE LOCATIONS. THEN PRAY THANKING GOD FOR PROMISES MADE TO JACOB AND US.

Pray: Asking God to help us trust fully in His promises always...

_____

Lesson written by Pastor Frank & Samuel Gervasi

_____

1. Adapted from *www.sermoncentral.com/sermonillustrations/77498/astor-s-promise-by-gordon-curley*, as accessed on 10/27/2024.
2. Quote by Charles Stanley, from *Charles Stanley Life Application Bible,* BibleGateway Plus, https://www.biblegateway.com/passage/?search=genesis%2028%3A11-15&version=NIV, as accessed on 03/20/2025.
3. *NIV Grace & Truth Bible.* BibleGateway Plus, *www.biblegateway.com*, as accessed on 3/20/2025.
4. New International Bible, Holy Bible, New International Version®, NIV® Copyright ©1973, 1978, 1984, 2011 by Biblica, Inc.® Used by permission. All rights reserved worldwide.

Going Deeper – Study Guide

Lesson: 24 – I Promise #2

Memory Verse: *"He was afraid and said, 'How awesome is this place! This is none other than the house of God; this is the gate of heaven.'"* **Genesis 28:17, NIV**

Open in Prayer:

Introduction:

There's a story about "a nurse living in the UK. At the healthcare facility where she works there is one patient with dementia who the nurse eats lunch with daily. The only problem is she's always afraid I won't come back. That I will forget her, Elizabeth said.....So, one day, Elizabeth wrote this patient a note, promising that she would remember to have lunch with her and not forget her. The patient took this note and placed it in her room. And in the days and weeks that followed, this patient would look at the note and remember the promise that was made if she forgot and began to worry."

1

Last Sunday, we began our focus on the life of Jacob, and God's promises to him. Today, we will see the importance of remembering God's promises, just like the elderly woman who looked at the note and remembered the promise made to her.

Read: *Genesis 28:13-17*

"There above it[a] stood the Lord, and he said: "I am the Lord, the God of your father Abraham and the God of Isaac. I will give you and your descendants the land on which you are lying. 14 Your descendants will be like the dust of the earth, and you will spread out to the west and to the east, to the north and to the south. All peoples on earth will be blessed through you and your offspring.[b]

Going Deeper – Study Guide

15 I am with you and will watch over you wherever you go, and I will bring you back to this land. I will not leave you until I have done what I have promised you." 16 When Jacob awoke from his sleep, he thought, "Surely the Lord is in this place, and I was not aware of it." 17 He was afraid and said, "How awesome is this place! This is none other than the house of God; this is the gate of heaven." (NIV)

Big Idea: *Sometimes We Must Reflect on God's Promises to Further Solidify Them in our Hearts.*

In verses 16 and 17, we see Jacob awake from his vision of the ladder, in which God had promised to bless Jacob and his descendants and be with him. And we can obviously see that this whole sequence of events has Jacob a little freaked out: *"When Jacob awoke from his sleep, he thought, 'Surely the LORD is in this place, and I was not aware of it.'* **He was afraid...**" (Genesis 28:16-17a, NIV; emphasis added)

1. **What Are Reasons Fear Can Be Strong at Times?** *(Explain)* _____

_____

_____

2. **Do You Think Fear and Anxiety Are the Same Thing?** *(Explain Your Answers)*

_____

_____

_____

3. **What Do the Following Verses Say About Fear?**

Genesis 9:2:	
Genesis 20:11:	
Exodus 9:30:	
Deuteronomy 2:25:	
Joshua 2:9:	

Going Deeper – Study Guide

The word *afraid* is also interesting and catches our attention, because it carries with it a few different meanings. It implies a combination of fright and alarm, and reverential fear. This combination shows us that Jacob was in full realization that the God of the universe, and the God of his own ancestors, had spoken directly to him.

Insight: *God is omnipresent – He is always everywhere, and this should lead us to be more in awe of him and trust Him even more to fulfill His promises to us.*

---

4. What Are Things That Cause People to Lose Their Awe of God? *(Be Specific)*

_____

_____

_____

5. What Steps Can We Take to Trust God More? *(Explain)* _____

_____

_____

Some people have described these verses as Jacob's conversion experience – when he finally stops running from God's plan for His life and begins to serve the Lord as his own God. Almost all of us can remember the day of our own conversion, and the way it causes us to reflect on what God has done and how He has spoken to us.

1 Samuel 12:14:	
1 Samuel 12:24:	
1 Chronicles 16:15:	
Acts 2:5:	
Acts 10:35:	

"Knowing that God is faithful, it really helps me to not be captivated by worry. But knowing that He will do what He has said. He will cause it to happen, whatever He has promised, thinking about it, then it causes me to be less involved in worrying about a situation." Josh McDowell 2

Going Deeper – Study Guide

Reflecting on and realizing who God is helps us to believe in the promises He makes, and remembering what He has done in the past helps us to keep believing when the waiting gets long. Jacob did these things, and it helped him understand the promise God had given him. And we should do the same thing.

Challenge
WHICH PROMISES OF GOD DO I NEED TO REFLECT ON? _____
_____
WHAT PROMISES DO I NEED TO REMEMBER? _____
_____
WHICH PROMISES HAS GOD FULFILLED IN MY LIFE? _____
_____

Going Deeper:

The **Wycliffe Bible Dictionary** defines the word *promise* as follows: *"While referring occasionally to a man's word. The characteristic use of 'promise' in Scripture is concerning what God declares he will bring to pass...God's first great promise to man is in Genesis 3:15 inaugurating the succession which, in growing clarity and detail right down to the annunciation, tells of the coming Messiah-Deliverer. A wide range of promises is connected more or less directly with this central promise, including the new covenant (Jer 31:31-34), the outpouring of the Spirit (Joel 2:28 f.), the restoration of Israel (Deut 30:1-5), and ultimately, new heavens and new earth (Isa 65:17; 66:22)...The technical term* **epangelia***, then, designates God's whole gracious commitment, expressed especially to Abraham [and passed on to Jacob], to perform His full redemptive work in Messiah, in whom 'all the promises of God are yea and amen' (II Cor 1:20)."* **3**

Going Deeper Challenge
MAKE A LIST OF THE PROMISES GOD HAS PROMISED TO FULFILL BUT HASN'T YET. THEN TRUN TIO HIM IN PRAYER SHOWING YOUR AWE AND REVERENCE

Pray: Asking God to help me remember His promises and solidify them in my mind...

_____

Lesson written by Pastor Frank & Samuel Gervasi

_____

1.   Adapted from https://becauseisaidiwould.org/i-will-come-back-for-lunch/; as accessed on 10/29/24.
2.   Josh McDowell, https://www.goodreads.com/author/quotes/4314.Josh_McDowell, as accessed on 10/29/2024.
3.   Wycliffe Bible Dictionary, by Charles F. Pfeiffer, Howard F. Vos, and John Rea. Copyright © 1999 by Hendrickson Publishers. All rights reserved.

Going Deeper – Study Guide

Lesson: 25 – Memorials in Context

Memory Verse: *"He called that place Bethel, though the city used to be called Luz."' Genesis 28:19, NIV*

Open in Prayer:

Introduction:

"Arlington National Cemetery, is the U.S. national burial ground in Arlington County, Virginia, on the Potomac River directly opposite Washington, D.C. The cemetery currently occupies 612 acres. The first soldier buried (May 13, 1864) on the Lee plantation was a Confederate prisoner who had died in a local hospital. Sixty-four other soldiers were also buried that day, including some in the estate's rose garden, and by the end of 1864 more than 7,000 soldiers had been interred. The cemetery subsequently became the burial ground for casualties from all U.S. wars since the American Revolution. Prominent soldiers and civilians have been buried at Arlington ever since serving as a memorial to remember them. " 1

Recently, we began our focus on the life of Jacob, and God's promises to him. Today, we will see the importance of remembering God's promises, and key encounters people have with Him by using memorials.

Read: *Genesis 28:16-19*

"When Jacob awoke from his sleep, he thought, "Surely the Lord is in this place, and I was not aware of it." 17 He was afraid and said, "How awesome is this place! This is none other than the house of God; this is the gate of heaven." 18 Early the next morning Jacob took the stone he had placed under his head and set it up as a pillar and poured oil on top of it. 19 He called that place Bethel,[a] though the city used to be called Luz." (NIV)

<u>Big Idea:</u> *Reminders are helpful—if they lead us to a deeper appreciation of God himself.*

Reminders are alright—if they lead us to a greater reverence of God and draws us closer to Him. Because in essence setting up reminders are ways to memorialize the event itself. Opportunities to think about and replay the encounter in our minds. And it's a good thing in most cases, if it leads us to a deeper appreciation about the promises *and* God.

1. ***How Do You Know if God is Making You a Promise?*** *(Explain)* _____

_____

_____

God's Promises will never contradict what's said in the Bible. So, if someone believes that God made them a promise that's not in the Bible. I would question the reality of it, always!

2. ***What Makes God's Promises So Hard to Wait on at Times?*** *(Be Specific)*

_____

_____

_____

In the case of Jacob, he does a couple of important but different things, doesn't he? Look starting in v. 18: *"Early the next morning Jacob took the stone he had placed his head under and set it up as a pillar and poured oil on top of it. He called that place Bethel though the city used to be called Luz."*

3. Look Up the following Verses and Highlight What Stands Out?

Genesis 9:15-16:	
Exodus 17:14:	
Numbers 15:39:	
Deuteronomy 16:3:	
1 Corinthains 11:24-25:	

Going Deeper – Study Guide

Looking back at Genesis, notice how Jacob does three different things to help remember as well. First, he used a bridge or tie, something that was from the actual event, like the *"stone" (vv.17, 18)* that he laid his head on. Probably so that when he saw it, he could recall it even more clearly, and what happened that day.

Second, he also consecrated the place meaning that he set it apart and had a mini ceremony where he could further memorialize it. Because Jacob then *"poured oil on top it."* *(v.18)* Which obviously *wasn't* doing it for prayer purposes but just another way that would cause him to remember the event further.

4. What Things Have You Kept Remembering Events in Your Life? *(Explain)*

_____

_____

_____

Insight: *Memorials are good but should never replace God or a person's relationship with God. In and of themselves they hold nothing unique, other than reflection.*

5. How Can We Consecrate Our Lives to God in a Greater Way? *(Be Specific)*

_____

_____

_____

Then lastly, renames the location, which was giving it that final, new identification. And the name itself *"Bethel"* means *"House of God." (v. 19),* which remained for many years in Israel with that name.

6. What Do the Following Verses Show About God?

Psalm 4:2:	
Psalm 40:4:	
Jeremiah 13:25:	
Jeremiah 16:19:	
Amos 2:4:	

However, earlier if you noticed, I said memorials are good in *some* cases. However, not in all instances, because they can have an undesired result also, especially, as they relate to matters of faith. That's because we want to be cautious that they don't replace God, going to Him in prayer, or that personal one-on-one time. Also, someone should be careful not to believe the memorial has some special power in and of itself. Like a statue or something like that, because they should cause us to deeper appreciation of the event or promise but not replace it.

"A pleasure is full grown only when it is remembering. You are speaking…as if pleasure were one thing and memory another. It is all one thing." (C.S. Lewis) 2

Challenge

WHAT MEMORIALS ARE IMPORTANT FOR ME TO REFLECT ON ABOUT GOD?
_____
_____
_____

WHICH MEMORIALS HAVE REPLACED MY TIME WITH GOD IN THE PAST?
_____
_____
_____

WHERE DO I TURN IN LIFE WHEN THINGS GET STRESSFUL OR CONFUSING? _____
_____
_____

Going Deeper:

The **NIV Application Commentary** comments on Genesis 28:12-16 as follows: *"When Jacob awakes, he has two responses. (1) He recognizes the nature of the place, which involves three steps. (a) He identifies the sacredness of the spot. Portals were associated with sacred space. It has already been noted that the ziggurats, representing portals, were constructed next to temples, which demarcated sacred space. Since Jacob has seen a portal here, he identifies the space as sacred space, a house of God. This house of God is at the earth end of the portal, whereas the other end of the portal is the gate of heaven.*

In Mesopotamian literature, the stairway led to the gate of the gods, and Jacob is thinking in those same terms. (b) Jacob sets up the stone as a pillar. Sacred pillars and standing stones are familiar in the religious environment of the ancient world. Archaeologists have found them in a variety of cultic settings dating from the fourth millennium to the first. They can be either natural or carved, inscribed or plain. The Canaanites used them (e.g., at the high place at Gezer), and they were found at the Israelite cultic installation at Arad. Anointing the pillar constitutes its dedication. Some of the standing stones that have been found include basins at their base for libations.* These stones are sometimes understood as the dwelling places of deity (houses of gods)." *3*

Pray: *Asking God, to help us remember your goodness to us always...*

Going Deeper Challenge
WHAT SEASONS OF LIFE DO I REMEMBER MOST ABOUT GOD WORKING IN? MAKE A LIST AND THEN SPEND TIME IN PRAYER THANKING HIM FOR HIS FAITHFULNESS....

Lesson written by Pastor Frank & Samuel Gervasi

Works Cited:

1. Adapted from https://www.britannica.com/place/Arlington-National-Cemetery; as accessed on 10/31/2024.
2. AZ Quotes, https://www.azquotes.com/quote/381374, as accessed on 10/31/2024.
3. NIV Application Commentary, Genesis, John Walton, Zondervan Academic 10/01/2000.

Lesson #26 – A Commitment of His Own

Memory Verse: *"'...then the LORD will be my God...'"* **Genesis 28:21b, NIV**

Open in Prayer:

Introduction:
One of the most important parts of a wedding ceremony is the "I do's", where each of the members of that marriage promise to love and stand by the other as a promise before God. To commemorate this pledge, the members of the marriage wear a ring on their fingers, to remind themselves of the commitment they are making.

In our devotion today, we conclude our focus on Jacob's encounter with God at Bethel. And we will see how the promises God had made prompts Jacob to respond with a promise of his own.

Read: *Genesis 28:20-22*

"Then Jacob made a vow, saying, "If God will be with me and will watch over me on this journey I am taking and will give me food to eat and clothes to wear 21 so that I return safely to my father's household, then the Lord[a] will be my God 22 and[b] this stone that I have set up as a pillar will be God's house, and of all that you give me I will give you a tenth." (NIV)

Big Idea: *God's Promises Should Lead Us to Commitment and Relationship.*

Going Deeper – Study Guide

In verse 20, we see that *"Then Jacob made a vow..."*. In this resolution, Jacob expresses his desire to serve God and follow Him if God will look after Jacob and keep the promises He had made in the vision. Our passage lists five small components of this promise Jacob makes before God. First, he asks God for provision. Remember that Jacob fled his home abruptly to escape his brother Esau's retaliation, so Jacob was declaring his dependence on the Lord to supply necessities like food and clothing.

1. ***What Are Reasons People Can Break Vows?*** *(Explain)* _____

_____

_____

2. ***What Are Some of the Vows or commitments You've Made to God in Past?*** *(Be Detailed)* **a.** _____

   b. _____ **c.** _____

   d. _____ **d.** _____

Jacob also asks for God's protection as he traveled alone through the wilderness. Subsequently, Jacob commits himself to personally serve Yahweh as his own God, as we see in verse 21b: *"...then the LORD will be **my** God..."* (NIV; emphasis added). Jacob had personally seen the glory of God, and he wanted in on a personal relationship with this God of promises.

3. ***What Do the Following Verses Show About Vows Made to God?***

Numbers 6:21:	
Job 22:27:	
Psalm 22:5:	
Psalm 50:14:	
Psalm 61:5:	
Psalm 61:8	

After Jacob commits himself to this personal relationship, he goes a bit further – promising not only to remember the promise God had made to him at Bethel, but also to give of his own treasures and resources as an offering to God: *"...and of all that you give me I will give you a tenth."* (v. 22)

4. **How Should knowing That God Wants to Be in Fellowship with Us Make Me Feel?** *(Be Specific)* _____
_____
_____

Insight: *God desires to have a personal relationship with each person — for them to be His children and be known by Him. He longs to be in fellowship with those who fear Him.*

5. **What Ways Can We Be in Fellowship with God?** *(Explain)* _____
_____
_____

6. **What Does the Following Scripture Show Us About Commitment?**

1 Kings 8:61:	
1 Kings 15:14:	
2 Chronicles 15:17:	
Acts 14:26:	

God desires for us to be committed to and in relationship with Him. And when He makes a promise to us, we should be moved to commit ourselves to Him in return. Because God is faithful to fulfill each one of His promises.

Challenge:
HOW DO I RESPOND WHEN GOD MAKES A PROMISE TO ME? _____
HOW CAN I SERVE AND FOLLOW HIM IN GRATITUDE TODAY? _____
HOW IS MY COMMITMENT TO THE LORD? _____
HOW CAN IT BE BETTER? _____

Going Deeper – Study Guide

Going Deeper:

Zondervan Illustrated Bible Backgrounds Commentary of the Old Testament says:
"Vows in the ancient world generally involved a request made of deity with a promise of a gift in return when the request is fulfilled. The request often concerned protection or provision, and the gift was typically a sacrifice or a donation to the sanctuary of the deity. The details in this chapter conform to that pattern. God has promised protection, provision, and return to the land, so Jacob makes those the condition of his proffered gift: a tithe of all that he acquires during his absence. Wealth and possession in the ancient world were not based on money, so Jacob expects to gain flocks and herds. Though tithes could at times be a form of taxation, this tithe is not imposed on Jacob. Gifts related to vows were usually given to the temple (whether by means of sacrifice or donation), but in this case it will have to be by, sacrifice because donations must be handed over to temple administrators, and there is no formal temple here. Jacob returns to Bethel to fulfill his vow in Genesis 35." 1

Going Deeper Challenge
LIST PROMISES GOD HAS MADE IN THE PAST TO YOU. THANK HIM IN PRAYER FOR HOW HE HAS PROVIDED....

Pray: *Asking God to care for me, and help me to serve Him considering His promises...*

_____

Lesson written by Pastor Frank & Samuel Gervasi

_____

Works Cited:

1.   Zondervan Illustrated Bible Backgrounds Commentary of the Old Testament, Copyright © 2002.

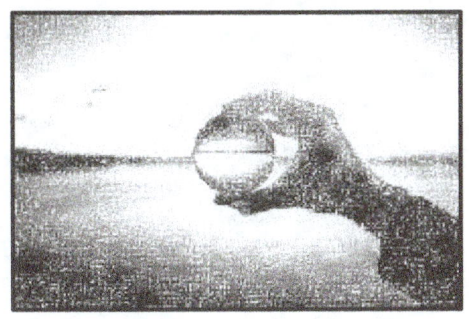

Lesson: 27 – In Focus

Memory Verse: *"Do you want to get well?" John 5:6, NIV*

Open in Prayer:

Introduction:

In our devotion today we're beginning a look at prayer. And we'll study a story about a man who needed God's healing. He was an invalid, for a very long time and had tried many times to do what some sick people were used to doing but had a hard time of it. In fact, we'll see some attitudes that are common, especially when it comes to change in people's lives or overcoming obstacles in a particular area of life.

Read: *John 5:1-15*

"Some time later, Jesus went up to Jerusalem for one of the Jewish festivals. 2 Now there is in Jerusalem near the Sheep Gate a pool, which in Aramaic is called Bethesda[a] and which is surrounded by five covered colonnades. 3 Here a great number of disabled people used to lie—the blind, the lame, the paralyzed. [4] [b] 5 One who was there had been an invalid for thirty-eight years. 6 When Jesus saw him lying there and learned that he had been in this condition for a long time, he asked him, "Do you want to get well?" 7 "Sir," the invalid replied, "I have no one to help me into the pool when the water is stirred. While I am trying to get in, someone else goes down ahead of me." 8 Then Jesus said to him, "Get up! Pick up your mat and walk." 9 At once the man was cured; he picked up his mat and walked. The day on which this took place was a Sabbath, 10 and so the Jewish leaders said to the man who had been healed, "It is the Sabbath; the law forbids you to carry your mat." 11 But he replied, "The man who made me well said to me, 'Pick up your mat and walk.' " 12 So they asked him, "Who is this fellow who told you to pick it up and walk?" 13 The man who was healed had no idea who it was, for Jesus had slipped away into the crowd that was there. 14 Later Jesus found him at the temple and said to him, "See, you are well again. Stop sinning or something worse may happen to you." 15 The man went away and told the Jewish leaders that it was Jesus who had made him well." (NIV)

Big Idea: *When trying to overcome obstacles we should pray with focus*

When facing a challenge, we should understand our obstacle (vv. 1-4.) Meaning that if we are going to change in any way, whether it's a big challenge or a small one, we need to understand what it is fully. Now in the case of the story the challenge was physical healing. But there were obstacles that lie in the mental arena that we're going to look at, as well. The location itself was called "Bethesda", depending on your version. However, v. 2 says, *"Now there is in Jerusalem near the Sheep Gate a pool, which in Aramaic is called Bethesda[a] and which is surrounded by five covered colonnades."*

1. **What Are Challenges That Can Arise When Faced with a Challenge?**
a. _____ b. _____
b. _____ d. _____

2. **What Mindsets Can Get in the Way of Overcoming Challenges in Life?** *(Explain)*
_____
_____
_____

Some have suggested it means *"House of mercy", (unknown).* However, it was one that Jesus knew well, because it was the place of the feeding of the 5000. As well as one of the disciples Phillip was from there. But also, in v.2 they mention a sheep gate. So, there was buying and selling of sheep, also a pool for watering sheep, probably the shepherds as well. So, you can kind of picture the surroundings, a little.

3. **What Do the Following Verses Show About Healing?**

2 Kings 2:18-20:	
2 Chronicles 28:15:	
Proverbs 2:18:	
Proverbs 16:24:	
Isaiah 58:8:	
Jeremiah 8:22:	

Going Deeper – Study Guide

However, also think about the atmosphere that was present, there were different obstacles. First, were many disabled people: meaning sick people were lying around. In fact, v. 3 says, *"A great number of sick people."* So, I think it might have been a little depressing, and kind of sad surroundings.

4. Do You Think Your Environment Has Affected Your Faith for God to Do the Miraculous in your Life? *(Be Detailed)* _____

_____

_____

The various levels of need are opportunities to show our faith in God. In today's passage he brings up a couple more. *"Here a great number of disabled people used to lie—the blind, the lame, the paralyzed. 5 One who was there had been an invalid for thirty-eight years.* Not to minimize any physical challenge but the blind was maybe the least dependent on others. Because they can still walk and do some things for themselves.

5. What Do the Following Verses Say About Healing and God?

Matthew 4:23:	
Luke 6:19:	
Luke 9:6:	
Acts 10:38:	
1 Corinthians 12:9:	
Revelation 22:2:	

However, the lame may have been only a body part or two not functioning. Nevertheless, the paralyzed were probably the worst of them because this may have been total in nature. Additionally, the length of need was long because v. 5 says, *"he had been invalid for thirty-eight years."*

6. Do You Believe God Can Heal Today? *(Explain)* _____

_____

_____

Going Deeper – Study Guide

Some schools of thought center around the healing done in the New Testament being only for the forming of the church. However, God still heals today in many ways and circumstances. The outcome is always up to Him. Additionally, the medical profession has gotten a bad rap. And God does sometimes to heal through traditional methods like a physician. God is the one giving doctor and scientists' wisdom and skill to be able to diagnose correctly. So, it's still God doing the healing if He chooses in that way. Faith in God will never be disappointed in His specific will for our lives.

Regardless of how big or difficult our challenges are in life; we should stay focused because God is able, and we can trust Him fully.

Challenge
HOW DO WE APPROACH THE CHALLENGES IN LIFE? _____ _____ _____ DO WE PRAY WITH FOCUS OR NOT? _____ _____ _____ IN WHAT AREAS HAVE WE DOUBTED THAT GOD COULD WORK? *(PHYSICAL OR NOT)* _____ _____ _____

Going Deeper:

Zondervan Illustrated Bible Backgrounds Commentary of the Old Testament says: *"A pool . . . called Bethesda (5:2). Public baths were standard in Greco-Roman cities, and people congregated there. A Qumran scroll attests the name of this pool (3Q15 11.12–13), and archaeologists have discovered a pool in this location fitting precisely this description. Although scholars do not all agree on the site of Bethesda (or its exact spelling), many favor a site under the Church of St. Anne in Jerusalem, just north-northeast of the temple. The pools were quite large (like a football field) and roughly twenty feet deep. This site had two twin pools, surrounded by four porches, or porticoes, and one porch (a fifth one) down the middle separating the pools (perhaps separating genders). Although John writes after Jerusalem was destroyed in ad 70, his recollection of the site is accurate."* **1**

Going Deeper Response
MAKE A LIST OF AREAS WHERE YOU NEED GOD TO DO THE SUPERNATURAL. THEN BRING THOSE THINGS BEFORE HIM IN PRAYER.

Going Deeper – Study Guide

Pray: *Asking God to give us focus and insight that can help give us faith when we pray...*

_____

Lesson written by Pastor Frank & Samuel Gervasi

_____

Works Cited:

1. Zondervan Illustrated Bible Backgrounds Commentary of the Old Testament, Copyright © 2002.

Lesson: 28 – The Seeds We Are Planting

Memory Verse: *"It is right for me to feel this way about all of you, since I have you in my heart and, whether I am in chains or defending and confirming the gospel, all of you share in God's grace with me."* **Philippians 1:7, NIV**

Open in Prayer:

Introduction:

When a boy came home from school one day, he found a neighbor's pickup truck backed up to his family's garden. Apparently, the boy's father had told the neighbor he could have the corn stalks for fodder. So, the young man got in the garden bed and helped pull the stalks out by the roots while he threw them into the truck bed. By the time they finished, the whole area looked like it had purposely been prepared for planting. So, the boy went and got a bag of peanuts that his grandmother had given him. He spaced them up and down the rows and ran out of peanuts right when he ran out of rows. Everything seemed perfect. However, it was not until after a thorough spanking by his father that it was made clear to him that the empty bed was not for the peanuts he had planted. The father had intended it for some other vegetable, but soon enough, that garden plot full of peanuts erupted into bloom. The yield produced an army cot piled high with peanuts to dry.

Read: *Philippians 1:1-11*

"Paul and Timothy, servants of Christ Jesus, To all God's holy people in Christ Jesus at Philippi, together with the overseers and deacons [a]: 2 Grace and peace to you from God our Father and the Lord Jesus Christ. 3 I thank my God every time I remember you. 4 In all my prayers for all of you, I always pray with joy 5 because of your partnership in the gospel from the first day until now, 6 being confident of this, that he who began a good work in you will carry it on to completion until the day of Christ Jesus. 7 It is right for me to feel this way about all of you, since I have you in my heart and, whether I am in chains or defending and confirming the gospel, all of you share in God's grace

with me. 8 God can testify how I long for all of you with the affection of Christ Jesus. 9 And this is my prayer: that your love may abound more and more in knowledge and depth of insight, 10 so that you may be able to discern what is best and may be pure and blameless for the day of Christ, 11 filled with the fruit of righteousness that comes through Jesus Christ—to the glory and praise of God." (NIV)

Big Idea: *Knowing Jesus and living for Him produces good fruit that glorifies God and builds others up.*

We may not be planting peanuts these days, but we are all planting seeds that produce fruit in the future. I heard one person say this: "That what we are on the inside, will always show on the outside."

1. What Types of Fruit Do You Think Are Consistent with Biblical Living? *(Be Specific)*

_____

_____

_____

2. What Types of Spiritual Fruit Have You Seen Produced in Your Life?

a. _____ b. _____

c. _____ d. _____

The church at Philippi was commended by the Apostle Paul for the fruit their lives were producing, in two primary areas.

For one, he praised them for helping him share the Gospel with others, using the phrase *"...your partnership in the Gospel..."* in verse 5. I like that because it shows a mindset that realizes that a church grows when the **entire** church body takes the responsibility of bringing others the Good News. And if you think about it, they were faithful in doing this, because he also uses the phrase "from the beginning." Which implies that their faithfulness in sharing the Gospel was over an ample period.

Going Deeper – Study Guide

3. What Do the Following Verses Show About Persevering in Matters of Faith?

Romans 5:11:	
2 Thessalonians 1:4:	
2 Thessalonians 3:5:	
Hebrews 12:1:	
James 1:3:	

4. What Are Reasons That Perseverance Might Be important in the Christian Life? *(Be Specific)* _____

_____

_____

The Deeper Our Troubles, the Louder Our Thanks to God, Who Has Led Us Through Them All & Preserved Us Until Today – Charles Spurgeon 1

The church at Philippi was also commended for their generosity. They were willing to use their financial resources that God had entrusted them for the furthering of God's work. The church at Philippi had previously sent gifts to the persecuted church in Jerusalem and had supported missionaries like Timothy and Epaphroditus. All these things showed their generosity.

__Insight:__   *Living life in obedience to God's commands is the best way to create a lasting impact in this world. As believers, we naturally begin producing "the fruit of righteousness" because Christ lives in us. But we still often need to choose to obey God and live out our faith.*

5. What Do the Following Verses Also Show About Perseverance?

James 5:11:	
2 Peter 1:6:	
Revelation 2:2:	
Revelation 2:19:	

The Apostle Paul responded to this fruit the church had demonstrated first by thanking God for them. Not just generally in passing, but "every time I remember you" (v. 3) and "for all of you." (v. 4) And finally, he prayed that *"...their love would abound more and more in knowledge and depth of insight..."* (v. 9) The church at Philippi had produced good fruit, but there was also room for growth. Even for us today, no matter how long we have been a Christian or how much we have grown in the past, none of us will arrive. We all need to continue growing and becoming more like Jesus. Paul was praying that Christ would continue working in their life. And in the end, they would bring glory to God, all because they were finding their identity in Him and producing the *"fruit of righteousness that comes through Jesus Christ to the glory and praise of God."* (v. 11)

"In Scripture the word 'seed' is used literally of the essential plant organism which enables the species to reproduce itself (Gen. 1:11)...It is also used in many figurative ways: of human offspring, descendants, and progeny (Gen. 3:15, 13:15); of 'the word of the kingdom' (Mt. 13:3-23); of 'the children of the kingdom of heaven' (Mt. 13:38); of 'the word of God' (Lk. 8:11; 1 Pt. 1:23); and of 'the kingdom of heaven' itself (Mt. 13:31-32)." **2**

Farmers Don't Plant Tomato Seeds and Expect Cucumbers...

Challenge
WHAT FRUIT IS MY LIFE PRODUCING? _____
_____
_____
DOES IT BRING GLORY AND PRAISE TO GOD OR NOT? _____
_____
_____
HOW CAN I CONTINUE TO GROW IN MY WALK WITH CHRIST? _____
_____
_____

Going Deeper – Study Guide

Going Deeper:

In the Apostle Paul's prayer in verse 9, he prays that the Philippians' love would abound **"more and more"**. This phrase gives us a picture of one step on top of another and on top of another. Which shows us this: **sanctification is not always instantaneous**. Positionally, we are "sanctified" and washed clean the moment we accept Christ. But the actual "how-to" and application is a process. Sometimes it's 2 steps forward and 1 step back. Sometimes it's 1 step forward and 2 steps back! But we must remember that we are a work in progress. Christ is still working in our lives to make us more like Himself. Be comforted today that, "...he who began a good work in you will carry it on to completion until the day of Christ Jesus." (v. 6)

Going Deeper Challenge
GRAB A PIECE OF PAPER AND LIST THE AREAS YOU HAVE GROWN IN SANCTIFICATION SINCE COMING TO CHRIST. NOW TURN THE LIST INTO A PRAYER OF THANKFULNESS TO GOD....

<u>**Pray:**</u> **Asking God to continue His good work in me, that I might bear fruit pleasing to Him...**

———————————

Lesson written by Pastor Frank & Samuel Gervasi

———————————————

<u>**Works Cited:**</u>

1. Charles Spurgeon Quotes, https://www.princeofpreachers.org/quotes/category/perseverance-of-the-saints, as accessed on 04/18/2025.
2. Wycliffe Bible Dictionary, pg. 1543, Charles F. Pfeiffer, Howard F. Vos, John Rea

Lesson: 29 – Who's the Person in the Mirror?

Memory Verse: *"Anyone who listens to the word but does not do what it says is like someone who looks at his face in a mirror and, after looking at himself, goes away and immediately forgets what he looks like." James 1:23-24, NIV*

Open in Prayer:

Introduction:

Warren Wiersbe tells in his book *Be Free* the fact that young pastors and ministers often visited the great British preacher G. Campbell Morgan. They would often ask him the secret of his success. Because it was said that he had a genuine and solid Christian faith. Morgan was said to reply, "I always say to them the same thing -- work; hard work; and again, work!" 1 And Morgan lived up to his own advice. He would be in his study every morning at 6 o'clock, finding rich treasures out of his Bible to pass on to God's people.

Read: *James 1:19-27*

"My dear brothers and sisters, take note of this: Everyone should be quick to listen, slow to speak and slow to become angry, 20 because human anger does not produce the righteousness that God desires. 21 Therefore, get rid of all moral filth and the evil that is so prevalent and humbly accept the word planted in you, which can save you. 22 Do not merely listen to the word and deceive yourselves. Do what it says. 23 Anyone who listens to the word but does not do what it says is like someone who looks at his face in a mirror 24 and, after looking at himself, goes away and immediately forgets what he looks like. 25 But whoever looks intently into the perfect law that gives freedom and continues in it—not forgetting what they have heard but doing it—they will be blessed in what they do. 26 Those who consider themselves religious and yet do not keep a tight rein on their tongues deceive themselves, and their religion is worthless. 27 Religion that God our Father accepts as pure and faultless is this: to look after orphans and widows in their distress and to keep oneself from being polluted by the world." (NIV)

Big Idea: *Practicing biblical commands is for all believers and should be practiced so each person can grow, avoiding hypocrisy.*

God wants us to strive for growth always practicing biblical principles and applying them to our lives. *"Brothers and sisters" (v. 19)* were terms that were reserved for Christ-followers. Sometimes people want to say that God will grow us as we pursue Him. And that's true but that should never be used as an excuse to NOT try, push, strive, and deliberately attempt to grow into a mature believer in Jesus Christ, especially areas that we can. Now, of course the areas that are difficult for us specifically, will require God's help through the Holy Spirit and prayer.

1. Which Commands in the Bible Do You Feel Are the Most Difficult to Follow? *(Explain)*

_____
_____
_____

2. Which Are the Easiest Commands to Follow? *(Give Your Reasoning)* _____

_____
_____

James lists several different areas that a mature life is shown. For instance, being a good listener *"Everyone should be quick to listen and slow to speak." (v. 19.)* He also lists controlling our temper, *"slow to become angry." (v. 19.)* As well as avoiding wicked behavior *"Therefore get rid of all moral filth and the evil that is so prevalent" (v. 21.)* All ways are characteristic of a person who is mature in faith.

3. What Do the Following Verses Say About Maturity in the Christian Life?

Luke 8:14:	
Ephesians 4:13:	
Colossians 1:28:	
Hebrews 5:14:	
James 1:4:	

Going Deeper – Study Guide

The reasons can be many for why we don't experience God's best in life. Sometimes the mindsets can be felt *like we can't grow* anymore or *not realizing when we don't* because of personal ignorance. Other times it may be *tiring to do good* when so many around us can be doing the opposite. Regardless of why though we can be sure God doesn't want us to deliberately avoid holiness and outwardly show others something different.

4. What Mindsets Have You Allowed to Hinder Your Faith in the Past? *(Be Specific)*

_____

_____

_____

Hypocrisy was always discouraged by Christ. James's style of writing was considered *in your face by some.* However, it may have been because he wanted Christians to practice what they were learning. Which could be seen in several ways in everyday interactions.

Insight: *Learning God's commands should be learned and applied always, so we can experience God's best. We should also avoid the mindsets that hinder our walk of faith.*

5. What Do the Following Verses Show About Hypocrisy?

Matthew 6:2:	
Matthew 7:4-6:	
Matthew 22:18:	
Mark 7:6:	
Luke 13:15:	

James also challenges others whether they were living out their faith in tangible ways like speech (v. 26,) helping the less fortunate (v. 27,) and maintaining a proper focus (v. 27) when he says, *"to keep oneself from being polluted by the World."*

A popular statement regarding how a Christian can reconcile the differences in how we should live biblically, and the culture around us is:

Be in the World but Not of it!   *(Unknown)*

Challenge

WHAT DO I SEE WHEN I LOOK AT MYSELF? _____
_____
_____

DOES MY LIFE ALIGN WITH HOW THE SCRIPTURES TEACH ME OR NOT? _____
_____
_____

HOW CAN I CONTINUE TO GROW IN FAITH? _____
_____
_____

Going Deeper:

Ancient biblical writers sometimes paralleled growth with everyday objects that people were familiar with. However, his use or comparison with a man looking in the mirror and forgetting what they looked like was a powerful one. The **NIV Cultural Backgrounds Study Bible** says, "*Some moral teachers recommended use of a mirror for moral reflection. Ancient mirrors rarely produced the more accurate images available today.*" **2** If that is true about the quality of mirrors in bible times, then James is possibly showing the lack of commitment to remembering biblical commands enough to apply them. We can assume that if we are to grow in faith, it will take effort on our part to be successful.

DESCRIBE WHAT YOU THINK PEOPLE SEE WHEN THEY LOOK AT YOUR FAITH. BE HONEST AND FAIR IN YOUR APPRAISAL...THEN COMMIT THE AREAS THAT NEED WORK TO GOD...

Pray: *Asking God to continue His work in the areas of my life, so my faith is being lived out....*

_____

Lesson written by Pastor Frank & Samuel Gervasi

_____

1.   Be Free, Chariot Victor Publishing, Copyright 1975.
2.   NIV Cultural Backgrounds Study Bible, Zondervan, Copyright 2016

Lesson: 30 - An Everlasting Reign

Memory Verse: *"The LORD will reign forever. He will be your God, O Jerusalem, throughout generations. Praise the LORD!"* **Psalm 146:10, NLT**

Introduction:

A gold sovereign is a type of coin minted in the United Kingdom, primarily between the years 1817-1914. The coin features on its face the image of Saint George (a Roman soldier in English mythology) on horseback, thrusting his spear into a dragon and saving others from danger.[1] Some gold sovereigns are valued at as much $376![2]

However, the word *sovereign* means more than just a type of obsolete British bullion. Sovereign also serves as an adjective, meaning *authority* and *jurisdiction*. Because a king has authority over and is in control of his kingdom and its citizens, that king is sovereign. But even the most powerful heads of state cannot begin to compare with the matchless authority and might of our Heavenly King. And we will see how that truth gives us ample reason to be grateful this Thanksgiving holiday.

Open in Prayer:

Read: **Psalm 146:10**

*"Praise the Lord. [a] Praise the Lord, my soul. 2 I will praise the Lord all my life;
I will sing praise to my God as long as I live. 3 Do not put your trust in princes,
in human beings, who cannot save. 4 When their spirit departs, they return to the ground; on that very day their plans come to nothing. 5 Blessed are those whose help is the God of Jacob, whose hope is in the Lord their God. 6 He is the Maker of heaven and earth, the sea, and everything in them—he remains faithful forever. 7 He upholds the cause of the oppressed and gives food to the hungry. The Lord sets prisoners free, 8 The Lord gives sight to the blind, the Lord lifts up those who are bowed down, the Lord loves the righteous. 9 The Lord watches over the foreigner and sustains the fatherless and the widow, but he frustrates the ways of the wicked. 10 The Lord reigns forever, your God, O Zion, for all generations. Praise the Lord." (NIV)*

Big Idea: *Because God is sovereign forever, He is worthy of our praise.*

In our passage, we see how the sovereign rule of God differs from that of human diplomats. Whereas every human ruler has an end to their reign, through one means or another, Yahweh is a King who will never be removed from His throne! Look at v. 10: *"The LORD will reign forever. He will be your God, O Jerusalem, throughout generations."* (NLT)

1. How Does God Reigning Supremely Make You Feel? *(Explain Your Answer)*

_____

_____

_____

2. How Would Define God's Sovereignty? *(Use a Dictionary if Necessary)* _____

_____

_____

Verse 10 highlights the greatest reason to be grateful – that God is in perfect control over everything, from the greatest trial to the richest blessing. And His sovereign authority extends even to the smallest details of our lives!

3. What Do the Following Verses Show About God?

Deuteronomy 33:27:	
1 Chronicles 16:36:	
1 Chronicles 29:10:	
Nehemiah 9:5:	
Psalm 41:13:	

David closes our Psalm by throwing in one final exclamation: *"Praise the LORD!"* (v. 10b, NLT) The Psalmist understood that God was in control, and it led to him giving God the praise He was worthy of. The same should be true of us, every day of our lives, but especially today. Because God has made it!

4. What About God Makes You Grateful? *(Be Specific)* _____

_____

_____

Going Deeper – Study Guide

5. What Are the Different Ways We Can Praise God? *(Be Creative)*

a. _____   b. _____
c. _____   d. _____

Luckily for us, that is not the case. God does reign in sovereignty and is perfectly in control of the entire universe. May we be a people that is so thankful, we praise the name of Jesus forever!

"If there is one single molecule in this universe running around loose, totally free of God's sovereignty, then we have no guarantee that a single promise of God will ever be fulfilled." – R.C. Sproul 3

Challenge
AM I GRATEFUL TODAY? _____   _____   _____
WHAT DO I NEED TO THANK GOD FOR? _____   _____   _____
RATE YOUR ATTITUDE CONCERNING GRATITUDE? (1-10) (EXPLAIN) _____   _____   _____

Going Deeper – Study Guide

Going Deeper:

Isn't it great news, not only that God will always reign on the throne, but as His children justified through Christ, we will reign with Him in future glory? In the **NKJV Wiersbe Study Bible**, Warren Wiersbe says this regarding Psalm 146:10:

"We 'reign' in life as, by faith, we draw upon our spiritual resources in Christ and together with Him make decisions and exercise ministry. We do not need to wait for the kingdom to come to start reigning with Christ (Matt. 19:28; Rev. 22:5), for God's grace is reigning now (Rom. 5:20, 21), and we can reign with Christ today (Rom. 5:21). Then we can have a life of praising God, trusting God, and loving God, a life that will glorify God."

Going Deeper Challenge
MAKE A COMPLETE GRATITUDE LIST. THEN THANK GOD VERBALLY FOR ALL THE WAYS HE IS WORTHY OF OUR PRAISE….

<u>Pray:</u>   *Thanking God for reigning in power and authority, and being in control of all things…*

———————

Lesson written by Pastor Frank & Samuel Gervasi

———————

Works Cited:

1. Adapted from https://www.chards.co.uk/guides/tails-the-designs-on-the-reverse-of-british-sovereigns/156, as accessed on 11/26/2024.
2. Adapted from https://www.bullionbypost.com/index/sovereign-guide/what-is-the-face-value-of-a-sovereign/, as accessed on 11/26/2024.
3. R.C. Sproul, taken from *Chosen by God: Know God's Perfect Plan for His Glory and His Children*.
4. Copyright © 2021 by Thomas Nelson. as accessed on Bible Gateway Plus, on 11/27/2024. All rights reserved.